Cape Town

Footprint

Francisca Kellett

Contents

Listings

About the author

Francisca Kellett first visited Africa as an anthropology student in the mid-1990s and has since found it hard to stay away. Although South Africa remains her preferred port of call, she has travelled extensively in southern and eastern Africa, straying occasionally as far north as Egypt and Morocco. A travel writer and photographer, her work has taken her from Brazil to Barcelona but she still swears that nowhere beats Cape Town. As well as being the author of this pocket guide, Francisca is the co-author of *Footprint South Africa* and has contributed to a number of other guidebooks. She writes regularly for the travel pages of newspapers and magazines and her photography has appeared in a range of travel guides. When not in Africa, she lives in the rather less exotic location of north London.

Acknowledgements

Thanks to Sheryl Ozinsky of Cape Town Tourism, Shaheema Hendricks of Western Cape Tourism, Rosie Wilkins in the London office of South Africa Tourism, and the excellent tourist offices at Stellenbosh, Hermanus, Franschhoek, Paarl and Wellington. I am indebted to Wessel Van Zyl and Annely Ickua, for their help with tours, festivals and nightlife, and to Lizzie Williams for her knowledge of the backpacker scene. A big thank you to Hugo Rifkind, Robert Dersley, Debbie Wylde at Footprint, Cate Henderson at Europcar, Hazel Smith at Kenya Air, Robin and the brilliant team at the Green Elephant Backpackers in Observatory and the staff at The Marine in Hermanus. Thanks also to the following readers who took the time to write in with their valuable comments and tips: John Roberson, Judith Safford, Mike and Eileen Christie, Petra and Marco Otto, Ansie and George von Mölendorff, Margot Quenstedt, Leslie Williams, Traudl and Franz Magerl, Maud McLeod, Jeffrey C Jennings, Jonathan Sleath and family, Yvette Baudewig, Michael Petersen, Ilya Marritz, Natasha Jooste, Aleksandar Djakovic, Inbar Benbenishty, Lieve Leroy, Alex Nikolic, Ian Wilkinson.

Cape Town is a city worth crossing the world for. First impressions simply don't get any better – the city is dominated by the stark splendour of Table Mountain, its steep slopes and flat top towering between the wild shores of the Atlantic. It is a city that is at once intense and laid back. The severity of the mountain is tempered by the soft, white sand of its beaches, the grand pomposity of its colonial buildings mollified by the buzzing markets that surround them. Its very nature seems audaciously fickle, evoking bafflingly conflicting images: notorious Robben Island and the body-beautiful hedonism of Clifton Beach; the call of the muezzin from the Bo-Kaap mosques mingling with the beats of funk and house in fashionable bars; the bronzed beach babe driving an open-top sports car past homeless, street-side families, opulent wine estates and the shanty towns of the Cape Flats. All of these images, however strange, are real and jostle for the visitor's attention.

Collective charisma

The main thing that will grab your attention is the people. Cape Town's population has an even greater collective charisma than Table Mountain, a mix of cultures, religions and ethnicities that drive the pulse of the city. Known as the 'Mother City' of South Africa, its uneasy past – seat of colonial rule, platform of apartheid and hotbed of political struggle – has done little to quench the communal vivacity that is so palpable in Cape Town today. The fabric of the city is undeniably energetic, from the waves that pound the shoreline to the countless festivals that fill the streets, yet Capetonians are renowned for their nonchalant attitude and come-what-may approach. This is the source of much contention for the rest of South Africa, which seems to fluctuate between despising Cape Town for its blasé and careless approach and applauding it for the very lifestyle that creates such an outlook. In typical Cape Town fashion, people seem little bothered by what outsiders think, content instead to bask in the reflected splendour of their city.

Cape capers

And who could blame them. This bewildering mix of environments and communities makes Cape Town an instantly likeable and captivating place. Around the city are some of South Africa's highlights, from the stunning natural beauty and historical Cape Dutch wine estates of the Winelands, to the pretty seaside resorts and superb whale watching of the Whale Coast. Few places in the world can offer mountain hiking and lazing on a beach in one morning, and tasting world-class wines or drinking home-brewed beer in a township *shebeen* in the evening. No big deal, you'll soon be thinking – just like a Capetonian.

At a glance

The city centre

The heart of Cape Town lies in a 'bowl' formed by a horseshoe of mountains – Signal Hill, Table Mountain and Devil's Peak – rolling down to the Atlantic. Cradled between the slopes and the sea lies the central business district, a compact grid of broad streets lined with a hotch-potch of modern high-rises and colonial buildings. Adderley Street is the main artery of the commercial centre, busy with a constant throng of shoppers, but at its southern end it turns into quiet, tree-lined Government Avenue which holds the city's major museums and historical buildings. A few blocks west lies quirky Long Street, backpacker central and a hive of trendy restaurants and late-night bars. Behind the centre, rolling up the southern slopes of the City Bowl, are the historical inner-city suburbs of Gardens, Oranjezicht and Tamboerskloof, affluent and leafy districts dominated by Table Mountain. To the west, on the slopes of Signal Hill, are the altogether different, but no less picturesque cobbled streets of the Bo-Kaap, the historical Muslim area which somehow survived apartheid's bulldozers.

Victoria and Alfred Waterfront

Northwest of the City Bowl lies Cape Town's original Victorian harbour, the city's most popular attraction. The whole area was completely renovated in the early 1990s, and today original buildings stand shoulder to shoulder with mock-Victorian shopping centres, al fresco restaurants and cinemas, all crowding along a waterside walkway with Table Mountain looming in the background. It is an enjoyable area, but very touristy – prices are higher in restaurants and shops, which some say are over-sanitized and artificial. Recent developments, however, such as the opening of the Nelson Mandela Gateway to nearby Robben Island, have gone some way in raising the area's cultural profile.

Atlantic Seaboard

Along the shore from the V & A Waterfront lies the modern residential area of Green Point, a bland throng of apartment blocks crowding between Signal Hill and the rocky shoreline, but hiding a huddle of colourful Victorian bungalows, known as De Waterkant Village. This has become Cape Town's major gay and lesbian hub, and the city's wildest bars and clubs stretch along the main Somerset Road. Following this road away from the City Bowl leads to Sea Point, a similarly modern coastal district with a sizeable Jewish population. In contrast to Green Point, however, Sea Point has a real family atmosphere and during the summer feels more like a European seaside resort than a South African suburb. Clifton, further round the peninsula from Sea Point, is Cape Town's take on Beverley Hills. This is where the rich and beautiful come to see and be seen, to show off bikinis and yachts, flex muscles and bask. Made up of a string of rocky coves, the small, white sand beaches are beautiful, backed by some of Cape Town's most sought-after villas and apartments, but surprisingly there is little in the way of nightlife or restaurants here. Camps Bay, just round the headland, has the monopoly on these. The main road stretching behind the long, more family-oriented beach is lined with some of the best seafood restaurants and 'sundowner' bars in Cape Town.

Southern Suburbs

On the other side of the City Bowl, stretching southeast along the slopes of Devil's Peak towards False Bay, are Cape Town's Southern Suburbs. The first suburb, Woodstock, is mainly a working-class coloured district, its rundown commercial centre hiding an attractive mesh of Victorian bungalows. Further along lies the bohemian hub of Observatory, an appealing grid of brightly painted houses, filled with trendy student-friendly bars, cafés and restaurants. The next suburbs of Mowbray, Rosebank and Rondebosch lie just below the University of Cape Town, getting progressively smarter (and whiter) as you progress round the mountain. Claremont, on the other side of Table Mountain, leads to beautiful Constantia, Cape Town's wealthiest suburb. Behind here, stretching up the slopes of Table Mountain, are the Kirstenbosch Botanical Gardens, a perfect backdrop to the heavily fortified mansions.

Cape Flats

The majority of Cape Town's inhabitants live in the townships of the Cape Flats, the vast plain stretching between Table Mountain and the Winelands. This is the first area that visitors pass through on their way from the airport to the city centre, but it is rarely visited by tourists and steadfastly avoided by white Capetonians. At first glance, the townships do seem barren and bleak, but beyond the imposing light towers and wire fences lie well-established and thriving communities, holding much of Cape Town's contemporary culture. The main townships – Guguletu, Langa, Mitchell's Plain, Crossroads and Khayelitsha – remain largely either coloured or black, and poverty and crime are a continuing scourge. Yet their pivotal role in the struggle against apartheid secured their importance in the life of Cape Town, and a visit to the townships provides a far broader sense of what the city is all about.

False Bay

On the other side of the peninsula from the city centre is False Bay, a vast arch stretching from the Cape of Good Hope to the headland before Walker's Bay and Hermanus in the east. False Bay is defined by a string of small seaside towns and fishing villages, including delightful Kalk Bay, an artsy village with the bay's only coloured fishing community, and well-established Simon's Town, the most family-oriented seaside settlement around Cape Town. Further south is famous Boulders Beach, with its entertaining colony of African penguins, and finally the Cape of Good Hope, a superb vantage point and excellent hiking country.

Trip planner

It would take months to take in everything Cape Town and its surroundings have to offer, but a week is enough to get a taster. Being on an exposed peninsula between two oceans means that Cape Town's weather is notoriously fickle. The winter months are cool and wet, but most weeks will have at least one day of bright sunshine. In summer temperatures can get well above 30°C, with perfect blue skies and cooling breezes, but this can change, with little warning, to fierce winds, horizontal rain and wild seas. Be prepared, therefore, to change your plans at the last minute.

Day one

A wonderful start and the best place to get a grip on Cape Town's layout is from the top of Table Mountain. A cable car whisks visitors to the summit offering astounding views. From here, head back down and take a taxi to Government Avenue. This delightful oak-shaded pedestrian road takes you past Company's Garden, some of the city's finest museums and colonial buildings. Head east to the superb District Six Museum, or wander towards Greenmarket Square.

Day two

The Victoria and Alfred Waterfront is a tourist-friendly development packed with shops, bars and restaurants and has an excellent aquarium. Stroll along the quays and watch seals cavorting in the water, or have a meal while watching the everyday life of a working harbour. The Nelson Mandela Gateway is here too, where you catch the ferry to Robben Island. Tours take three hours and provide an insight into the Machiavellian workings of the apartheid system.

Day three

To explore the great outdoors, take a drive to the Cape of Good Hope, a beautifully wild area offering panoramic ocean views and good walks as well as a couple of wild beaches perfect for a picnic. Drive back along the False Bay Seaboard and stop off at Boulders Beach, a haven for a huge colony of African penguins. They are amazingly nonchalant about humans, and you can get very close and watch them waddling about their business.

Day four

Spend half a day exploring the Southern Suburbs which stretch around Table Mountain. The obvious highlight is the Kirstenbosch Botanical Gardens. They are amongst the finest in the world and stunning, not least due to their setting, creeping up the slopes of Table Mountain. Similarly beautiful is the wealthy area of Constantia with its lush setting and excellent vineyards. In sharp contrast are the nearby Cape Flats, an enormous spread of townships and shanty towns. They are best visited on a tour which takes half a day.

Day five

The Whale Coast is a true highlight during the late winter and spring months, when huge numbers of Southern Right whales come into the bays to calve. Hermanus, just an hour from Cape Town, is hailed as having the best land-based whale watching in the world. You could come here for a day trip, but it is a pleasant spot to spend a night by the sea.

Day six

Spend a lazy day at one of the beaches on the Atlantic Seaboard. These are some of the most beautiful in the world – perfect arches of white sand washed by turquoise water. Camps Bay and Clifton have the added advantage of being frequented by Cape Town's movers and shakers, making them perfect for a few hours of people watching. Alternatively, drive around the mountain to False Bay, with its pretty towns, child-friendly beaches and warm waters. Both seaboards have an excellent choice of seafood restaurants, perfect for a large, end-of-holiday meal.

★ **Ten of the best**

Best

1 **Table Mountain** Take the cable car to the top and marvel at the spectacular views over the city, p31.

2 **Kirstenbosch Botanical Gardens** Stroll through the magnificent gardens and picnic in one of the most beautiful settings in South Africa, p63.

3 **Robben Island** Visit the notorious prison where Nelson Mandela was held for 18 years and learn about the struggles of political prisoners during apartheid, p51.

4 **Company's Gardens and Government Avenue** Wander through the beautiful gardens and leafy avenue in the heart of the city, lined with historical museums and colonial buildings, p33.

5 **District Six Museum** Visit Cape Town's finest museum, exploring the devastating effects of apartheid on local communities, p42.

6 **Cape of Good Hope Nature Reserve** Explore the rugged tip of the peninsula at Cape Point and climb to the superb views of False Bay and the Atlantic, p58.

7 **Boulders Beach** Watch the colony of African penguins waddling and squabbling about their daily business at Boulders Beach, p73.

8 **Clifton** Bronze your limbs with the rich and beautiful at Cape Town's most exclusive beach, p54.

9 **Whale watching in Hermanus** Head to Hermanus, an hour from Cape Town, for some of the finest whale watching in the world, p79.

10 **Winelands** Spend a day touring the beautiful valleys of the Winelands, trying South Africa's best wines at historical estates, p85.

Contemporary Cape Town

Cape Town is an unquenchably optimistic city. Although still recovering from decades of white minority rule, Capetonians have an unwavering belief in a bright and promising future. This upbeat and easy-going nature has long defined the city. Locals are noticeably friendlier and more laid back than in other parts of the country, and the streets and markets buzz with a confident energy. But it is its exceptionally varied population that distinguishes Cape Town first and foremost – the term 'Rainbow Nation' seems more appropriate here than anywhere else.

Certainly, Cape Town's population is the most cosmopolitan in the country. It has a comparatively small black African population – about a third of the total – while the distinctive 'Cape coloured' community makes up over half of the population. These are descendents of slaves brought from India, East Africa and Madagascar who interacted with European and local indigenous people, and today comprise much of the city's middle class. The third largest group is made up of white descendants of Dutch and British settlers, but there is also a sizeable Asian community.

Whatever their origins, Capetonians are fiercely proud of their city, and go about life with a certain boisterousness that is both sneered at and envied by the rest of South Africa's urban population. A long-standing rivalry remains between Johannesburg and Cape Town – a sort of New York/LA thing, where Capetonians envy Jo'burg's strong economy, and Jo'burg craves Cape Town's location and relaxed way of life. While Jo'burg residents are seen as sophisticated but, in essence, dull, Capetonians are perceived as hungover hippies who spend far too much time on the beach. The fact that Cape Town is invaded every summer by tens of thousands of Gauteng dwellers, however, seems to say a lot.

Jealousies aside, much of Cape Town's character has been sculpted by its rich diversity of languages. Afrikaans and English are most commonly heard, although the increasing black population is bringing Xhosa to the forefront. Afrikaans is the main language of Cape Town's coloured population, as well as being a major player in the identity of white Afrikaners. Although there are fewer of the latter in Cape Town than in other parts of the country, the Winelands is a major focal point of Afrikaner culture. Their distinctive Cape Dutch architecture, at its best on the historical wine estates around Stellenbosch and Paarl, remains the most celebrated in South Africa. Afrikaans is a creolized version of Dutch – the result of the interaction between Cape Town's slave and colonial cultures. In the townships of the Cape Flats, Afrikaans is spoken with a dialect known as *Kapie-Taal*, with English and Xhosa words thrown in to produce a distinctive combination which is evolving fast into a new language. The Cape Flats are in fact a hotbed of new developments in the life of the city. Music is a major focal point everywhere in Cape Town, but much of it originates here, particularly distinctive Cape Jazz.

Religion is similarly varied, with strong Christian, Muslim and Jewish communities, as well as those following African traditions. Perhaps the best-known of Cape Town's religious groups is known as the Cape Malays, the Muslim community focused on the Bo-Kaap. The term Cape Malay, however, is a misnomer – in reality a very small percentage of the population originated in Malaysia. Islam was instead introduced from India, Indonesia and East Africa, from slaves brought in by the Dutch East India Company in the 16th and 17th centuries. Today, the Muslim community retains a strong identity, which does much to define Cape Town's diverse religious scene. Nevertheless, despite the rich mix of cultures that makes up the city's population, many still identify themselves by, and live according to, race.

Such sentiments remain largely an issue of geography and economics. The Group Areas Act of the 1960s ensured that all prime land was in white hands – districts in the centre of town, by the seaside or along the lush slopes of Table Mountain, while coloured and black communities were, often forcibly, resettled in townships on the bleak and barren Cape Flats. The devastating urban planning of the apartheid era segregated all residential areas by race. The official barriers may have long since disappeared and residential boundaries are shifting, but districts are by and large still defined by colour. This can mean that the visitor gains a lopsided view of Cape Town – experiencing the ordered, affluent city that barely hints at the grinding poverty found in less visible parts.

Economics, too, play a crucial role. The division between rich and poor remains – put simply, the most affluent sector is white and the poorest black. Thankfully, this is changing: in the decade since the end of apartheid, a significant black middle class has emerged, and the coloured middle class is strengthening. Certainly, Cape Town is keen to shift thoughts regarding race and colour. The term coloured, for example, has been rejected by some as inappropriate in a post-apartheid South Africa, while others have proudly reclaimed it as a symbol of their distinct culture and history.

However people define themselves, Capetonians seem unanimously proud of their city. Apartheid's hangover is far from gone, but there is an strengthening sense of celebration of Cape Town's many different faces, a move towards applauding cultural differences – rather than airbrushing them out of history. In the ten years since democracy first took hold, Cape Town, more than anywhere else in South Africa, has learned to revel in its 'Rainbow Nation' label.

Travel essentials

There are frequent direct flights to Cape Town from most European countries, the United States, Australia and neighbouring African states. The cost of a ticket can be expensive – the city is becoming more and more popular, and prices can be correspondingly high. Booking as far in advance as possible, however, can bring prices down considerably.

Like much of South Africa, Cape Town lacks a decent public transport system. Thankfully, most of the city's oldest buildings, museums, galleries and the commercial centre are concentrated in a relatively small area. There is a bus network which travels between the city centre and the Southern Suburbs, but it can be slow and tiring. Faster and more efficient are the minibus taxis which are generally safe to use. Taxis are affordable and the local rikki taxis can be very good value for the major sights and backpacker lodges. To get the most out of the city and to visit the suburbs, beaches, Winelands and Whale Coast, it's a good idea to rent a car.

Getting there

Air

From Europe Although flights between Europe and Cape Town are long haul, they are surprisingly easy. Flights usually last about 12 to 13 hours, and are always overnight, but the main advantage is that there is no jetlag – the time difference is only +2 GMT. **British Airways** and **South African Airways** are the two main flight operators, but all of the major European carriers serve Cape Town (usually via other cities, such as Amsterdam or Frankfurt), often at very competitive prices. During peak season, a direct return flight can cost as much as £1,200, but if you book several months in advance, this can drop to below £500. Prices drop further if you choose an indirect flight. European carriers such as **Lufthansa** and **KLM** often have good value offers with return flights from £450, although these travel via another European city and often stop off at Johannesburg. **Virgin Atlantic** offers competitive flights to Cape Town from London Heathrow, and **Kenya Airways** operates flights between London and Cape Town, or Johannesburg, via Nairobi.

From North America **South African Airways** runs direct flights from Atlanta to Cape Town (daily except Fridays), and from New York JFK to Cape Town, via Johannesburg (daily). Flight time is around 17 hours, with prices hovering near the £850 mark in peak season. **American Airlines** has a code-sharing agreement with *British Airways*, making it possible to fly from major US airports to Cape Town via London. Prices start at £700, and the flight time is about 19 hours in total, although stop-over time in London can be up to 12 hours. **Delta Airlines** has a more convenient agreement with *South African Airways*, with daily non-stop flights between JFK and Johannesburg, with onward connections to Cape Town. Alternatively, there is a daily flight from JFK to Cape Town via Atlanta. Fares vary widely, but are usually in the range of £700-1,400,

Airlines

American Airlines, T 1800-4337300, www.aa.com
British Airways, T 0870-8509850 www.britishairways.com
Delta Airlines, T 1800-2211212 , www.delta.com
KLM, T 0870-5074074, www.klm.com
Lufthansa, T 0845-7737747, www.lufthansa.com
Qantas, T 0845-7747767, www.qantas.com
South African Airways, T +27 (0)11-9785313 , **T** 0870-7471111
www.flysaa.com
Virgin Atlantic, T 0870-2202464 www.virgin-atlantic.com

Discount flight agents

Bridge the World, T 0870-4432399, www.bridgetheworld.com
Flightbookers, T 0870-0107000, www.ebookers.com
The Flight Centre, T 0870-4990040, www.flightcentre.co.uk
STA Travel, T 0870-1600599, www.statravel.co.uk
Trailfinders, T 020-7983 3939 www.trailfinders.com
Travelbag, T 0870-9001351, www.travelbag.co.uk

and the flight time is around 17 hours. **United Airlines** work with *Lufthansa*, offering daily flights via Frankfurt from Washington, but note that there is a long stop-over in Frankfurt.

From Australia and New Zealand **Qantas** has a code-sharing agreement with *South African Airlines*, and between them they run regular flights from Sydney and Perth to Johannesburg, with onward connections to Cape Town. Flights run approximately four times a week with prices from £600, although they can be double this during peak season. Flight time is around 11 hours. **Singapore Airlines** offers regular direct flights between Sydney and Johannesburg, and has a code-sharing agreement with *Air*

New *Zealand* (which means that flights from New Zealand to Cape Town have three stops, including Johannesburg).

Airport information   Cape Town International Airport is a modern airport with convenient shops, car rental and travel agents desks. International long haul flights are always overnight, which means they arrive at a reasonable time in the morning.
The International and Domestic terminals are a 20-minute drive from the city centre, a 22-km trip. Expect to pay up to R300 for a taxi to the centre of town – they should have a special airport licence and must use their meter by law. It is better value to get one of the shuttle buses that operate the route, which you can organize in advance or from the airport: **Magic Shuttle**, **T** 021-9345455; **Way To Go**, **T** 021-9342503; **City Hopper**, **T** 021-9344440.

Getting around

Bus
The Waterfront bus, run by Golden Arrow, runs from Cape Town railway station to the Victoria and Alfred Waterfront and costs R2.50 one-way. It runs every 15 minutes. Generally, though, bus services are slow and best avoided.

Car
Although the main sights in central Cape Town are within walking distance of each other, it's a good idea to hire a car for a couple of days to get to the beaches and Kirstenbosch or Cape Point. Parking is generally not a problem. Most of the centre has demarcated areas, costing R6 per hour. There are official parking attendants (in blue uniforms) who patrol the centre – they'll ask how long you want to stay and you hand them the coins. Petrol prices are reasonable and there are plenty of large petrol stations around the city. Note that none are self-service and you must pay in cash. At quiet times car hire prices should be considerably cheaper than

around December and January. The cheapest local car hire companies change frequently – it's a good idea to check at backpacker hostels to see which ones they recommend. Although roads are in good condition and driving is usually hassle-free, bear in mind that drink-driving is commonplace despite it carrying heavy penalties. People drive fast and overtaking on blind corners is the norm. It's best not to drive at night – stick to taxis.

Cycling

Despite Cape Town's outdoorsy vibe, suprisingly few people get about by bicycle. There are few cycle lanes in the city and the frenetic driving of many motorists can make it unsafe. However, cycling as a sport is very popular and mountain biking in particular has taken on in a big way. In March, Cape Town is host to the world's largest timed cycle race, a mammoth trail skirting around False Bay and over the mountains to the city. Much of the area around Cape Town is very well suited to mountain biking, with good trails around Table Mountain as well as several popular routes criss-crossing the Winelands. See Sports, p202, for details of companies that provide bike hire and organize mountain biking trips.

Minibus taxis

These serve all areas of the city on fixed routes, and leave from the minibus terminal accessed from the top floor of the Sanlam Golden Acre shopping centre on Adderley Street. They can also be flagged down from the street. Minibuses to the Atlantic coast usually leave from outside *OK Bazaars* on Adderley Street. Most trips cost R3. They stop running at 1900. Unlike in some South African cities, these are generally safe to use, although avoid anywhere outside of the city centre, do your best not to look like a tourist and leave all valuables at home.

Rikki taxis
These small shared people-carriers are a good value alternative to getting around the city. You need to call one, but they pick up several people along the route, bringing down costs.

Taxis
There are several ranks dotted around town – the most useful ones are outside the train station at Adderley Street, by the *park inn* hotel on Greenmarket Square, and on Long Street. You can also flag down any that you see cruising around. If you are outside the city centre, you will have to call one in advance. Be sure to get a quote as prices can vary a lot. Companies change regularly, so either ask your hotel or restaurant to call one for you, or ask at the Tourist Office for reliable numbers, **T** 021-4264260.

Train/metro
Metrorail serves the suburbs. Services run as far as Simon's Town, but also go out as far as Worcester. We have received conflicting reports as to how safe these trains are, but it's a good idea to only travel first class; each station has signs as to where the first class carriage will be when the train comes in. Avoid using the trains at any times other than rush hour, usually between 0700-0800 and 1600-1800. Train times change seasonally, so check with Metrorail (**T** 0800-656463) for the latest timetable information. Trains start running around 0500, then approximately every 15 mins between the city centre and Simon's Town, until around 1900. Tickets cost R12 for a single.

Walking
Thankfully, most of the city's oldest buildings, museums, galleries and the commercial centre are concentrated in a relatively small area and best explored on foot. Most of the key sites are an easy stroll from each other – Long Street, Government Avenue, Adderley Street, Greenmarket Square and the Castle of Good Hope

→ Travel extras

Money
The South African currency is the Rand (R) which is divided into 100 cents (c). As long as you have the right type of card and sufficient funds, using an ATM (Automatic Teller Machine) is the most convenient and cheapest way of obtaining funds.

Safety
Cape Town has had problems of crime directed at tourists in the past, but this has improved significantly in recent years. Many of the problem areas now have CCTV cameras in the streets, and private security guards protect shops, restaurants and hotels. The most simple points to remember are: avoid carrying valuables and conceal cameras; don't walk around areas you're not familiar with; try not to look like a tourist; don't walk anywhere other than the busiest areas late at night; and make sure you do not drive in rural areas after dark. If you are going to be travelling alone in a car, it's advisable to take your mobile phone or hire one.

Tipping
Waiters, hotel porters, stewards, chambermaids and tour guides will expect a tip – 10-15% is an acceptable average.

Vaccinations
South Africa requires yellow fever vaccination certificates from travellers who have entered from other (especially Central and West) African countries. There is no malaria in the Western Cape.

Visas
All visitors are issued with temporary visitor permits lasting 90 days.

are all within a 20-minute radius. The V & A Waterfront is a bit of a walk away, and really only accessible by car, bus, or the Convention Centre canal. The beaches, suburbs and the Cape of Good Hope are all inaccessible by foot, so it's a good plan to hire a car.

Tours

City centre tours
Cape Town Tourism owns the Explorer Bus, a double-decker topless bus which follows a 2-hr route around the city. Contact the main tourist office for details, **T** 021-4264260, www.cape-town.org. Hylton Ross offers **Topless Tours**, **T** 021-5111784, a 2-hr city tour.

Cultural tours
Grassroute Tours, **T** 021-7061006, www.grassroutetours.com, specializes in township tours beginning in District Six and continuing to Langa and Khayelitsha, also a history of Cape Muslims tour. This company works with the communities it visits, putting back some of the proceeds. Half-day tours cost around R300. **Tana-Baru Tours**, **T** 021-4240719, conduct specialist tours of the Cape Malay Quarter lasting two hours. Led by Shereen Habib, they are interesting and good value. Expect to pay about R150 per person including a typical Cape Malay meal in a private home. Also offers township tours lasting three hours. **Cape Capers**, **T** 083-3580183, tourcape@mweb.co.za Cultural tours led by Faisal Gangat who won the 'Tourist Guide of the Year' award in 2003. Range of trips, from half-day tours looking at Cape Town's slave history to District Six and Bo-Kaap tours.

Boat tours
Condor Charters, **T** 021-4185806, offer harbour tours in a luxury motor yacht, fully equipped for private parties, which leaves from Quay 4. **Tigger Too**, **T** 021-7905256, www.tigertoo.co.za, departs from the Waterfront for sunset cruises and day trips. Fishing can be

organized but booking is advised during peak periods. **Drumbeat Charters**, T 021-7914441, Hout Bay, offer daily trips around Cape Point and to Duiker Island. **Nauticat**, T 021-7907278, www.nauticatcharters.co.za, runs daily cruises around Hout Bay and to see the seals at Duiker Island. The **Waterfront Boat Company**, Quay 5, V&A Waterfront, T 021-4185806, www.waterfrontboats .co.za, has six boats to choose from including a large catamaran and astylish yacht, and offers a range of boat tours including around Robben Island, whale watching, sunset and dinner cruises.

Coach tours
Day Trippers, T 021-5114766, www.daytrippers.co.za, runs small-scale bus tours to Cape Point, the Winelands, Township tours or the Whale Coast. Good value and fun, popular with backpackers. **Hylton Ross**, T 021-5111784, www.hyltonross.co.za, is the best-known coach tour operator, with an excellent range of well-organized trips. Some examples include city tours and trips to the Winelands, Cape Point, False Bay and Hermanus. 10 per cent of fees go towards the Tourism Community Development Trust (www.tcdtrust.org.za). **Easy Rider Wine Tours**, T 0218864651, stumble@iafrica.com, offer hugely popular day-long wine tours aimed at backpackers, organized by the *Stumble Inn* (see Sleeping). Tours take in five estates, with five tastings in each, restaurant, lunch and cheese tasting included (R225 all inclusive) although they seem to take too many people making it rather chaotic.

Whale Coast tours
Coastal Kayak Trails, T 028-3410404, www.kayak.co.za, offers various routes and guided kayak tours. **Dyer Island Cruises**, T 082-8018014, www.dyer-island-cruises.co.za, runs boat trips to Dyer Island. **Southern Right Charters**, T 082-3530550 (cell), seascapes@hermanus.co.za, are a boat-based whale-watching company. **Walker Bay Adventures**, just out of town towards Gansbaai at Prawn Flats, T 028-3140925,

Township tourism

A popular tourism initiative in the city has been 'Township Tourism', where houses (and in some cases shacks) in the townships of the Cape Flats have been opened to tourists. While this allows visitors to experience this lesser-seen side of Cape Town and get a feel for township life, it also provides much needed tourist dollars in underprivileged areas. One of the best places to stay for a night or two is **Vicky's B&B**, **T** 021-3877104, or vickysbandb@yahoo.com, in Khayelitsha, run by the welcoming Vicky. Her self-built house has two simple, clean double rooms, and she cooks excellent meals and can organize visits to local schools and nights out in the nearby *shebeen*.

wbadventures@hermanus.co.za, has all types of boats for hire, including canoes, rowing boats and pedaloes, plus fishing equipment. Daily cruises on the lagoon for larger groups and the ever-popular sundowner cruise are also on offer.

Tourist information

Cape Town Tourism, The Pinnacle, corner of Burg and Castle sts, **T** 021-4264260, F 4264266, www.cape-town.org   *Open Mon-Fri 0800-1900, Sat 0830-1400 and Sun 0900-1300*. This is the main, official city tourist office and can help with bookings and tours throughout the Western Cape. It is an excellent source of information and a good first stop in the city. In addition to providing practical information about Cape Town, it can help with accommodation bookings and has plenty of information on nightlife and events. This is also the site of **Western Cape Tourism, T** 021-4625639, www.capetourism.org, and there is a **South Africa National Parks** desk, www.parks-sa.co.za. There's also a café, gift shop and internet access. The other branch of Cape

Town Tourism is in the Clock Tower Centre at the **Victoria & Alfred Waterfront**, **T** 021-4054500, *daily 0900-2100*.

For information on the **Wine Routes**, get in touch with the Stellenbosch Wine Route office, **T** 021-8864310, www.wineroute.co.za *Mon-Fri 0830-1300, 1400-1700*. The Paarl Wine Route office, **T** 021-8723605, www.paarlwine.co.za, is also a good source of information with an excellent website outlining the local wine estates.

Hermanus Tourism Bureau, Old Station Building, Mitchell Street, **T** 028-3122629, www.hermanus.co.za   *Mon-Fr 0800-1800, Sat 0900-1700, Sun 0900-1500 (shorter hours in winter)*. The office is extremely helpful and has information on the whole region, plus a room dedicated to booking accommodation.

Table Mountain 31 The mountain makes Cape Town what it is.

The city centre 32 A mish-mash of modern high-rises, beautiful colonial buildings, African markets, peaceful gardens and museums.

Victoria and Alfred Waterfront 53 Full to the brim with restaurants, bars and shops, it is also home to the impressive aquarium and the Nelson Mandela Gateway to nearby Robben Island.

Atlantic Seaboard 59 This is the peninsula's most spectacular stretch of coast with the Twelve Apostles providing a rugged backdrop. Each beach has its own character, from body-beautiful to family-friendly.

Southern Suburbs 68 Once largely the enclave of affluent whites, today there is an interesting mix of cultures and two of Cape Town's finest attractions: Kirstenbosch Botanical Gardens and Constantia.

False Bay 74 The bay is a string of seaside resorts and fishing villages that have a distinct family feel. It's a bit twee but the droves of penguins and the chance of seeing whales compensate.

★ Table Mountain

Cape Town is defined, first and foremost, by Table Mountain. The centre of the city nestles beneath it, and it seems almost rude not to make it your first stop. Being whisked to the summit by cable car and taking in the spectacular views is without doubt a highlight, and an excellent introduction to the layout of the city and the astounding variety of environments found on the peninsula.

T 021-4248181, www.tablemountain.net Latest mountain weather reports **T** 021-4245148. Mountain Rescue **T** 021-9489900. *Daily 0830-2000/2200 (last car down at 1900 in winter). R95 adult return, discounts for children. The tourist office shuttle bus to the Lower Cable Car leaves every half hour from the main office on Burg St and costs R30. Taxis cost R50-60 from the city centre.* Map 1, C3, p246

Rising a sheer 1,073 m from the coastal plain, the mountain dominates almost every view of the city, its sharp slopes and level top making it one of the world's best-known city backdrops. For centuries, it was the first sight of Cape Town afforded to seafarers, its looming presence visible for hundreds of kilometres. Its size continues to astonish visitors today, but it is the mountain's wilderness, bang in the middle of a bustling conurbation, that makes the biggest impression. Table Mountain sustains over 1,400 species of flora, as well as baboons, dassies (large rodents) and countless birds. Watch out for the 'Table Cloth', the impressive layer of flat cloud that descends on the top of the mountain most afternoons, its edges wafting down the highest slopes.

It is worth going to the top for the dizzying trip in the cable car alone. The two cars carry up to 65 passengers each, and have

! For the perfect coffee-table-book photo of Table Mountain, drive 25 km north of the city to Bloubergstrand. The broad beach gives perfect views of Table Bay and the mountain.

★ **Sunset spots**

rotating floors allowing for a full 360 degree view. The average journey time is three minutes. There is a bistro restaurant and souvenir shop at the top station, as well as a cheaper café. From here, a range of paths wind across the rocky top, each leading to different viewpoints over the peninsula.

The area stretching from Table Mountain to Cape Point was recently proclaimed as the **Table Mountain National Park**, and the mountain itself is protected as a national monument. For many years there were only a few known paths to the top, but today there are an estimated 500. One of the easier popular routes starts from Kirstenbosch Botanical Gardens and takes about three hours to get to the top. However, even busy routes should not be taken lightly. Given Table Mountain's size and location, conditions can change alarmingly quickly and the mountain has claimed its fair share of lives. The weather may be clear and calm when you set out, but fog and rain can descend without warning. Before venturing out, ensure that you have suitable clothing, waterproofs, plenty of food and water and a mobile phone. Inexperienced hikers, or those interested in learning more about the mountain's flora and fauna, should take a guide or a walking tour.

● *Lion's Head is an easier, alternative climb offering stunning 360 degree views. It takes two hours and is popular at full moon to watch the sunset and descend by the light of the moon. Signal Hill, further along, is accessible by car, has equally spectacular views and is perfect for watching sunset with a sundowner in your hand.*

The city centre

The city itself rolls from the lower slopes of Table Mountain and holds most of Cape Town's major sights and attractions. From the Lower Cableway Station, you look out over the **City Bowl**, the central residential suburbs of Tamboerskloof, Gardens, Oranjezicht and Vredehoek, and beyond here lie the high-rise blocks of the business district. Closest to the mountain is **Oranjezicht**, a quiet district with a good selection of places to stay. **Vredehoek**, on the other hand, is characterized by a cluster of ugly high-rise apartments. **Gardens** is a lively neighbourhood on the fringes of the city centre, with a good choice of restaurants and guesthouses. Cape Town's best-known hotel, the Mount Nelson, is situated here.

From here the land slopes gently towards the Waterfront, with the commercial heart of the city laid out in between. From the magnificent tree-lined **Government Avenue** and the oasis calm of **Company's Gardens**, the city opens up into a lively hub of broad streets buzzing with a medley of besuited executives, trendy media types and boisterous market sellers. This is the historical heart of the city, but also the commercial centre, and as such is a mish-mash of beautiful colonial buildings, modern office blocks and crowded shopping precincts. **Adderley Street** is the main artery, with most sights a few blocks away. The superb **District Six Museum** and the **Castle of Good Hope** are a few blocks to the east; **Long Street**, the playground of the young and hip is a short stroll west, with the lively market at **Greenmarket Square** lying between.

▶▶ See Sleeping p103, Eating and drinking p129, Bars and clubs p161

 Sights

Government Avenue and Company's Gardens
Free. Map 2, B7/C7, p249

Government Avenue is an oak-shaded pedestrian route running past Company's Gardens, a clutch of museums and the grand, bright-white Houses of Parliament. Company's Gardens, situated on the site of Jan van Riebeeck's original vegetable garden, was created in 1652 to grow produce for settlers and ships bound for the East, see p43. It is now a small botanical garden, with lawns, a variety of labelled trees and ponds filled with Japanese koi. The grey squirrels living amongst the oak trees were introduced by Cecil Rhodes – Cape Prime Minister from 1890-96 – from America. There are also a couple of statues here: opposite the South African Public Library at the lower end of the garden, is the oldest statue in Cape Town, that of Sir George Grey, Governor of the Cape from 1854-62. Close by is a statue of Cecil Rhodes, pointing northwards, with an inscription reading, "Your hinterland is there", a reminder of his ambition to paint the map pink from the Cape to Cairo. There is a café in the garden, serving drinks and snacks beneath the trees.

South Africa Museum and Planetarium
Company's Gardens, **T** 021-4813800, www.museums.org.za/sam *Daily 1000-1700. R10, free for kids and all day Sun. There's a shop and café in the museum. Planetarium shows, Mon-Fri 1400, Sat and Sun 1300, 1430, late showing on Tue 2000. R20, R6 for kids. Map 2, C6, p248 See also Kids, p215*

This is the city's most established museum, specializing in natural history, ethnography and archaeology, and is a good place to take children. There are extensive displays of the flora and fauna of southern Africa, including the popular Whale Well, where you can listen to the sound of whale song, but the highlight is the new permanent 'IQe – the Power of Rock Art' exhibition. The displays of ancient San rock art have been in the museum for almost a hundred years, but following a process of consultation and dialogue with Khoi-San communities, they have been re-interpreted in a far more sensitive and illuminating manner. The exhibits focus on the significance and symbolism of San rock art, with some fascinating examples including the beautifully preserved Linton panel, which depicts the trance experiences of shamans. The whole exhibition, although short, is beautifully arranged and accompanied by recorded San singing, a disjointed and haunting sound. Nearby are the ethnographic galleries, offering interesting displays on the San, Khoi and Xhosa, amongst others, as well as the original Lydenburg Heads. A soon-to-open addition to the natural history section is 'Shark World', an interactive multi-media area exploring the world of sharks. At the Planetarium next door presentations change every few months, but a view of the current night sky is shown on the first weekend of each month. The shows are fascinating and last an hour.

Bertram House

Government Av, **T** 021-4643280. *Open Mon by appointment only. R5. Map 2, D6, p248*

This early 19th-century red brick Georgian house has a distinctly English feel to it. The building houses a collection of porcelain, jewellery and English furniture, the majority bequeathed by Ann Lidderdale, a Capetonian and important civic figure in the city in the 1950s. Downstairs the two drawing rooms contain all the trappings of a bygone elegant age – card tables, a Hepplewhite settee, a square piano and a fine harp. Three rooms have wallpaper from London, a very expensive luxury for the period. Upstairs the Doris Tothill silver tea set and the hair jewellery are particularly fine.

Jewish Museum

88 Hatfield St, **T** 021-4651546, www.sajewishmuseum.co.za *Sun-Thu 1000-1700, Fri 1000-1400. R30, R10 for kids. Closed on Jewish and public holidays. Map 2, D7, p249*

In 1841 a congregation of 17 men assembled for the first time in Cape Town to celebrate Yom Kippur. At the meeting they set about the task of raising funds to build a synagogue, and in 1862 the foundation stone was laid for the first synagogue in southern Africa. The following year the building was completed and furnished – quite a feat for such a small community at the time. Inside the newly renovated museum is a rich and rare collection of items depicting the history of the Cape Town Hebrew Congregation and other congregations in the Cape Province. On display upstairs are bronze Sabbath oil lamps, *Chanukkah* lamps, *Bessamin* spice containers, *Torah* scrolls, *Kiddush* cups and candlesticks. There is a beautiful stained-glass window depicting the Ten Commandments in Hebrew. From here a glass corridor leads you to a newer section of the museum which is devoted to the history of Jewish immigration to the Cape, mainly from Lithuania. A lot of thought has been put into the displays, which include photographs, immigration certificates, videos and a full reconstruction of a Lithuanian *shtetl* or village. The museum complex also houses a library, café and bookshop.

Holocaust Centre

88 Hatfield St, **T** 021-4625553, www.museums.org.za /ctholocaust *Sun-Thu 1000-1700, Fri 1000-1300. Donation. Map 2, D7, p249*

Cape Town's newest museum is also one of its best, comprising an intelligent and shocking examination of the Holocaust. Exhibits follow a historical route, starting with a look at anti-Semitism in Europe in previous centuries, and then leading to the rise of Nazism in Germany, the creation of ghettos, death camps and the Final Solution, and liberation at the end of the war. Video footage, photography, examples of Nazi propaganda and personal accounts of the Holocaust produce a vividly haunting display. The exhibits cleverly acknowledge South Africa's emergence from apartheid and draw parallels between both injustices, as well as looking at the link between South Africa's Greyshirts (who were later assimilated into the National Party) and the Nazis. The local context is highlighted further at the end of the exhibition, with video accounts of Jews who survived the Holocaust and moved to Cape Town.

National Gallery
Government Av, **T** 021-4674660, www.museums.org.za/sang
Tue-Sun 1000-1700. R10, kids free. Map 2, D7, p249

The National Gallery houses a permanent collection of local and international art, as well as some interesting temporary exhibitions. Of some interest is the collection of 18th- and 19th-century British sporting paintings donated by Sir Abe Bailey, but more diverting are the changing exhibitions of contemporary South African art. These have recently included 'Decade of Democracy', a comprehensive visual record of the last decade, with work on display by celebrated local artists Willie Bester, Marlene Dumas, Zwelethu Mthethwa and Berni Searle.

Rust en Vreugd
78 Buitenkant St, **T** 021-4643280, www.museums.org.za/rustvreugd
Open Mon by appointment only. Map 2, D8, p249

A few hundred metres east of the National Gallery, hidden behind a high whitewashed wall, is this 18th-century mansion. It was declared a historical monument in 1940, and subsequently restored to its best period. Today it houses six galleries displaying a unique collection of watercolours, engravings and lithographs depicting the history of the Cape. Commercial exhibitions are held in the galleries upstairs.

South African Public Library
Queen Victoria St, **T** 021-424632, www.ulsa.ac.za *Mon-Fri*
0900-1700. Map 2, B7, p249

Adjoining the gardens is the South African Public Library, behind St George's Cathedral. Opened in 1818, it is the country's oldest national reference library and was one of the first free libraries in the world. Today it houses an excellent and important collection of historic books covering South Africa. The building also has a bookshop and an internet café.

Houses of Parliament
Government Av, **T** 021-4032537. *Map 2, B8, p249*

On the other side of the avenue stands the Houses of Parliament, completed in 1885, and the seat of national parliament since 1910 when the Union was formed. In front of the building is a marble statue of Queen Victoria, erected by public subscription in honour of her Golden Jubilee. It was unveiled in 1890 by the then Governor, Sir Henry Loch. While parliament is sitting, from January to June, it is possible to watch from the visitors' gallery during the week and to take guided tours of the chambers and Constitutional Assembly, but you must phone ahead to check times and bookings.

St George's Cathedral
Corner of Government Av and Wale St. *Map 2, B8, p249*

The last building on Government Avenue is St George's Cathedral, best-known for being Archbishop Desmond Tutu's diocese from 1986 until 1996. It is from here that he led over 30,000 people to City Hall to mark the end of apartheid, and where he coined the now universal term 'Rainbow nation'. The building you see today is comparatively new: it was built at the beginning of the 20th century, after the first church, based upon St Pancras Church in London, was turned down. The present cathedral was designed by Sir Herbert Baker.

Slave Lodge

Corner of Adderley and Wale sts, **T** 021-4608240,
www.museums.org.za/slavelodge   *Mon-Fri 0830-1630,
Sat 0830-1300. R10, kids R3.   Map 2, B8, p249*

Slave Lodge, previously known as the Cultural History Museum, is
the second oldest building in Cape Town and has had a varied
history, starting life as a lodge for slaves, and then becoming a
library, a post office, the Cape Supreme Court, and finally a
museum in 1966. Its most significant role, however, was as a slave
lodge for the VOC (Dutch East India Company). Between 1679 and
1811 the building housed up to 1,000 slaves. Local indigenous
groups were protected by the VOC from being enslaved; slaves
were consequently imported from Madagascar, India, Indonesia
and other parts of Africa, creating the most culturally varied slave
society in the world.

Conditions at the lodge were terrible and up to 20% of the
slaves died every year. Sadly only a glimpse of this history is
displayed in the museum. Instead, there are changing temporary
exhibitions on the ground floor, focusing on the culture and
history of the VOC. The top floor houses a muddle of British and
VOC weapons, household goods, furniture and money, as well as
relics from Japan and ancient Rome, Greece and Egypt. The
museum's planners have been in the process of restructuring the
museum for several years now, so it remains to be seen if it
develops into an exploration of the history and lasting effects of
slavery – as many hope it will.

Groote Kerk

Corner of Adderley and Spin sts.   *1000-1400, weekdays. Free guided
tours available on request.   Map 2, B8, p249*

Nearby is one of Cape Town's older corners, Church Square, site of
the Groote Kerk. Up until 1834 the square was used as a venue for

the auctioning of slaves from the Slave Lodge, which faced onto the square. All transactions took place under a tree – a concrete plaque marks the old tree's position.

The Groote Kerk was the first church of the **Dutch Reformed** faith to be built in South Africa – building started in 1678 and it was consecrated in 1704. The present church, built between 1836 and 1841, is a somewhat dull grey building designed and built by Hermann Schutte after a fire had destroyed most of the original building. Many of the old gravestones were built into the base of the church walls, the most elaborate of which is the tombstone of Baron van Rheede van Oudtshoorn. Two of the Cape's early governors are buried here – Simon van der Stel (1679-99) and Ryk Tulbagh (1751-71). Of particular note is the beautiful pulpit carved by Anton Anreith, whose work can also be seen at Groot Constantia. The two baroque heraldic lions which support the pulpit are said to represent the power of faith.

● *Look out for the rows of pews with their own locked doors. These belonged to wealthy 19th-century families who didn't want to pray with commoners.*

City Hall and Grand Parade
Darling St. *Map 2, B9, p249*

From Adderley Street, a short walk down Darling Street takes you to the City Hall and the Grand Parade. The latter is the largest open space in Cape Town and was originally used for garrison parades before the Castle was completed. Today the oak-lined parade is used as a car park and twice a week it is taken over by a busy market. After his release from prison, **Nelson Mandela** made his first speech to over 100,000 people on the Grand Parade from the City Hall on 9 May 1994. This neo-classical building was built to celebrate Queen Victoria's Golden Jubilee. It is now headquarters of the Cape Town Symphony Orchestra and houses the City Library. The library reading room has local, national and international newspapers.

Castle of Good Hope

Darling St, **T** 021-7871082, www.castleofgoodhope.co.za
*0900-1600. R18, includes a free guided tour (1100, 1200 and 1400).
Map 2, B10/11, p249*

Beyond the Grand Parade is the main entrance of South Africa's oldest colonial building, the Castle of Good Hope. Work started in 1666 by Commander Zacharias Wagenaer and was completed in 1679. Its original purpose was for the Dutch East India Company to defend the Cape from rival European powers, and today it is an imposing sight, albeit a rather gloomy one. Under the British, the Castle served as government headquarters and since 1917 it has been the headquarters of the South African Defence Force.

Today the castle is home to three museums. The **William Fehr Collection** is one of South Africa's finest displays of furnishings, reflecting the social and political history of the Cape. There are landscapes by John Thomas Baines and William Huggins, 17th-century Japanese porcelain and 18th-century Indonesian furniture. Upstairs is an absurdly huge dining table which seats 104, in a room still used for state dinners.

To the left of the Fehr Collection is the **Secunde's House**. The Secunde was second in charge of the settlement at the Cape, responsible for administrating the Dutch East India Company. The three rooms do not contain original furniture from the Castle, but they do recreate the conditions under which an official would have lived in the 17th, 18th and early 19th centuries.

The third museum is the **Military Museum**, a rather indifferent collection depicting the conflicts of early settlers. More absorbing are the regimental displays of uniforms and medals. The free guided tours are informative and fun, although a little short. Tour highlights include the torture chambers, cells, views from the battlements and Dolphin Court, where Lady Anne Barnard was supposedly seen bathing in the nude by the sentries. While waiting for a tour you can enjoy coffee and cakes at a small café, or explore van der Stel's restored wine cellars, where you can taste and buy wines. There is full ceremonial Changing of the Guard at noon.

★ District Six Museum
25a Buitenkant St, **T** 021-4618745, www.districtsix.co.za   *Mon 0900-1500, Tue-Sat 0900-1600. Donation.   Map 2, C9, p 249*

Housed in the Methodist Church, this museum is one of Cape Town's most powerful exhibitions and gives a fascinating glimpse of the stupidity and horror of apartheid. District Six was once the vibrant, cosmopolitan heart of Cape Town, a largely coloured inner city suburb renowned for its jazz scene. In February 1966, PW Botha, then Minister of Community Development, formally proclaimed District Six a 'white' group area. Over the next 15 years, an estimated 60,000 people were given notice to give up their homes and moved to the new townships on the Cape Flats. The area was razed, and to this day remains largely undeveloped, although the government recently handed over the first pocket of re-developed land to a small group of ex-residents and their descendants. What the area will become remains to be seen – the issue remains controversial as many ex-residents feel the open, barren land should remain as a poignant testimony to the forced removals.

The museum contains a collection of photographs, articles and personal accounts depicting life before and after the removals. There are usually a couple of musicians at the back, tinkering away at their guitars and tin pipes and adding immeasurably to the atmosphere of the place. Highlights include a large map covering most of the ground floor, upon which ex-residents have been encouraged to mark their homes and local sights. The 'Namecloth' is particularly poignant: a 1.5 m-wide length of cloth has been provided for ex-residents to write down their comments, part of which hangs by the entrance. It has grown to over 1 km in the last eight years, and features some moving and insightful thoughts. A new display in the back room looks at the forced removals from the Kirstenbosch area.

Adderley Street and Heerengracht
Map 2, B8/A9, p249

Adderley Street is one of the city's busiest shopping areas, and is sadly marred by a number of 1960s and 70s eyesores, but it does still boast some impressive bank buildings. On the corner of Darling Street is the **Standard Bank Building** (1880), a grand structure built shortly after the diamond wealth from Kimberley began to reach Cape Town. The exterior has a central dome surmounted by the figure Britannia, but it is the main banking hall which is of most interest, with all the original Victorian features remaining largely intact. Diagonally across Adderley Street is the equally impressive **Barclays Bank Building** (1933), a fine Ceres sandstone building which was the last major work by Sir Herbert Baker in South Africa.

At the corner of Adderley Street and Strand Street stands a modern shopping mall complex, the **Sanlam Golden Acre**. On the lower level of the complex the remains of an aqueduct and a reservoir dating from 1663 can be viewed. The line of black floor tiles close to the escalator which links the centre with the railway station mark the position of the original shoreline before the reclamation work began in Table Bay. Continuing down towards the docks, Adderley Street passes Cape Town Railway Station. At the junction with Hans Strijdom Street is a large roundabout with a central fountain and a bronze statue of **Jan van Riebeeck**, given to the city by Cecil Rhodes in 1899. Reibeeck was the first European to settle at the Cape, arriving in 1652 with 90 others. At the bottom end of Adderley Street are statues of Bartholomew Dias, a Portuguese

! Cape Town is booming as a film location on account of the settings, perfect light and low costs. Adderley Street is often used to depict modern shopping streets in US cities and the famous unfinished flyover at the end of Buitengracht is a favourite spot for movies and TV advertisements.

explorer who was the first European to reach the Cape of Good Hope in 1487, and Maria van Riebeeck, wife of Jan van Riebeeck, donated respectively by the Portuguese and Dutch governments in 1952 for Cape Town's tercentenary celebrations.

In front of the Medical Centre on Heerengracht is the **Scott Memorial**. What is on show is in fact a bronze replica; the original, a stone argosy, was smashed by vandals. Its location has barely changed, but when it was unveiled in 1916 it was on the approach to a pier at the foot of Adderley Street, a further indication of how much additional land has been reclaimed from Table Bay over the years. The palm trees once graced a marine promenade in this area. Up until the 1850s there was a canal running the full length of Heerengracht and Adderley streets. This was covered over as the city prospered and traffic congestion became a problem.

Koopmans-De Wet House
Strand St, **T** 021-4242473, www.museums.org.za/koopmans *Open Mon by appointment only. R5. Map 2, A8, p249*

Just off St George's Mall, on a pedestrian road lined with shops and cafés, is the delightfully peaceful Koopmans-De Wet House. Surviving in the midst of ugly modern buildings and the bustle of central Cape Town, the house is named in memory of Marie Koopmans-De Wet, a prominent figure in cultured Cape Society who lived here between 1834 and 1906. The inside has been restored to reflect the period of her grandparents who lived here in the late 18th century. Though not too cluttered there is a fascinating collection of furnishings which gives the house an appealing, tranquil feel.

● *Look out for the 'Bart of Africa' sculpture on St George's Mall, The three-metre bronze of an African tourist curio is randomly covered with heads of cartoon character Bart Simpson, and has been cause for considerable debate in the city.*

Gold of Africa Museum

96 Strand St, **T** 021-4051540, www.goldofafrica.com *Mon-Sat 1000-1700. R20. Map 3, H10, p251*

A few blocks west of Koopman's-De Wet House is the Lutheran Church and Martin Melck House, now home to the Gold of Africa Museum. Originally the house served as a clandestine Lutheran church, as in the 18th century the Dutch authorities refused to tolerate any churches other than those belonging to the Dutch Reformed Church. The present museum is a slick presentation of the history of gold mining, outlining the first mining by Egyptians in 2400 BC and the subsequent development of trade networks across Africa. There are comprehensive displays of 19th and 20th century gold artworks from Mali, Ghana and Senegal, including jewellery, masks, hair ornaments and statuettes. It's a reasonably diverting collection, but you need a real interest in precious metals to stay for long. Downstairs there's a café and workshop where you can watch goldsmiths do their thing.

Greenmarket Square

Map 2, A8, p249 See also Shopping p195

This is the old heart of Cape Town and the second oldest square in the city. It has long been a meeting place, and during the 19th century it became a vegetable market. In 1834 it took on the significant role of being the site where the declaration of freeing all slaves was made. Today it remains a popular meeting place and is lined with outdoor cafés and restaurants. A busy daily market sprawls across the cobbles, with stalls selling African crafts, jewellery and clothes.

Most of the buildings around the square reflect the city's history. Dominating one side is the *park inn* hotel, housed in what was once the headquarters of the Shell Oil Company – note the shell motifs on its exterior. Diagonally opposite is the **Old Town**

House (1751), originally built to house the town guard. It became the first town hall in 1840 when Cape Town became a municipality. Much of the exterior remains unchanged, and with its decorative plaster mouldings and fine curved fanlights is one of the best preserved Cape Baroque exteriors in the city. Today the white double-storeyed building houses the **Michaelis Collection** of Flemish and Dutch paintings (Mon-Fri 1000-1700, Sat 1000-1600). Next to the *Tudor Hotel* is the second oldest building in the square – the **Metropolitan Methodist Church** (1876). This is the only high Victorian church in Cape Town and has a tall spire with a unique series of miniature grotesques decorating its exterior.

● *If you're interested in antiques, walk out of the square past the Methodist church to Church Street. The area between Burg and Long streets is the venue for a daily antique street market.*

Long Street
Map 2, B6-A8, pp248-249 See also Bars and clubs p161

This stretch is one of the trendiest in Cape Town and is something of a nightlife hot-spot. Lined with street cafés, fashionable shops, bars, clubs and backpacker lodges, it has a distinctly young feel about it, but is also home to some fine old buildings. One of Cape Town's late Victorian gems is at number 117, now an antique shop. On the outside is an unusual cylindrical turret with curved windows; inside is a fine cast iron spiral staircase leading to a balustraded gallery.

Slave Church Museum, at number 40, is the oldest mission church in South Africa, built between 1802-04 as the mother church for missionary work carried out in rural areas. Though utilized bydirectors and members of the South African Missionary Society, it was more commonly used for religious and literacy instruction of slaves in Cape Town. By 1960 most of its congregation had been moved to the Cape Flats. Inside, there is a permanent display of missionary work throughout the Cape, and behind the pulpit are display cabinets showing early cash accounts and receipts for the transfer of slaves.

★ The Bo-Kaap
Map 2, p248

A few blocks west along Wale Street is the Bo-Kaap, Cape Town's historical Islamic quarter and one of the city's most interesting residential areas. The area was developed in the 1760s and today feels a world away from the nearby CDB. Here the streets are cobbled and tightly woven across the steep slopes of Signal Hill, the closely packed houses painted in Smartie colours. Although fast becoming popular with a yuppie class, the area has managed to retain much of its ambience and strong identity. Bo-Kaap residents are descendants of slaves imported by the Dutch in the 17th century – although they are still sometimes referred to as Cape Malays, only a tiny percentage originated in Malaysia. Most came from India, Madagascar and West Africa. **Bo-Kaap Museum**, (**T** 021-4243846, Tue-Sat 0900-1600, R5) housed in an attractive 18th-century house, is dedicated to the community and contains the furnishings of a wealthy 19th-century Muslim family. There are antique furnishings and Islamic heirlooms such as an old Koran and *tasbeh* beads set in front of the mihrab alcove, while the back room has displays dedicated to the input that slaves had on the economy and development of Cape Town. The photos are the most interesting exhibits, giving a fascinating glimpse of life in the Bo-Kaap in the early 20th century. At the back is a community centre, with temporary photographic exhibitions. The house itself is one of the oldest buildings in Cape Town surviving in its original form. It was built by Jan de Waal for artisans in 1763 and it was here that Abu Bakr Effendi started the first Arabic school and wrote important articles on Islamic Law. He originally came to Cape Town as a guest of the British government to try and settle religious differences amongst the Cape Muslims.

Victoria and Alfred Waterfront

*Cape Town's original Victorian harbour is the city's most popular attraction. The whole area was completely restored in the early 1990s, and today it is a lively district packed with restaurants, bars and shops. Original buildings stand shoulder to shoulder with mock-Victorian shopping centres, museums and al fresco restaurants, all crowding along a waterside walkway with Table Mountain looming in the background. Until very recently, the Waterfront was seen as something of a hedonistic playground for tourists – the only reason for coming here was to shop and eat, and many argued that the area was over-sanitized and artificial. While it certainly remains touristy, recent developments have changed its image somewhat. The opening of the **Nelson Mandela Gateway** to nearby **Robben Island**, with a museum depicting prison life, has gone some way in raising the area's profile. It is also becoming known as an outdoor music venue, hosting live acts during the annual **Jazz Festival**. And despite being geared towards tourists it remains a working harbour, which provides much of the area's real charm.*

▸▸ *See Sleeping p108, Eating and drinking p135*

 ## Sights

Clock Tower

Map 3, C11, p251. See also Robben Island, p51

A number of original buildings remain around the basins and are an interesting diversion from the razzmatazz of the shops and restaurants. At the narrow entrance to the Alfred Basin, on the Berties Landing side, is the original Clock Tower, a red octagonal Gothic-style tower built in 1882 to house the Port Captain's office. It stands in front of the Clock Tower Centre, the newest collection of shops, offices and restaurants on the Waterfront, with a helpful tourist office on the first floor. Next door is the **Nelson Mandela Gateway to Robben Island**, from where you catch the main ferry to the island. The ultra-modern Gateway has photographic and interactive displays on apartheid and the rise of African nationalism on the first floor, *open 0730-1800, free entrance.*

Union Castle Building
T 021-4195957. *Tue-Sun 0900-1800. R10. Map 3, C10, p251*

Walking across the swing bridge from the Clock Tower (look out for the frolicking Cape fur seals as you cross), you come to the *Victoria and Alfred Hotel.* Opposite here is a stocky square building known as Union Castle Building (1919), designed by the firm of architects owned by Sir Herbert Baker. The Union Steamship Company and the Castle Line both ran monthly mail ships between Britain and South Africa, in the late 19th century. In 1900 they amalgamated and from then on mail was delivered every week. The last Union Castle ship to sail to England with the mail was the *Windsor Castle* in 1977.

Victoria and Alfred Hotel
Dock Rd. *Map 3, C10, p251*

Opposite the Union Castle Building is this luxury four-star hotel. It was originally built as a coal store before being converted into Union Castle's warehouse and customs baggage store. It had a third floor but this was destroyed in a fire in 1939. This building is a perfect example of how effective restoration can be, and how with a bit of imagination a whole area can be given a new lease of life.

! The area derives its name from the two harbour basins
● around which it developed. Construction began in 1860, when Prince Alfred, Queen Victoria's second son, tipped the first load of stone to start the building. Alfred Basin could not handle the increased shipping so Victoria basin was built.

This was the first hotel to be opened at the Waterfront and it is an important part of the success of the whole venture.

Time Ball Tower
Dock Rd. *Map 3, C10, p251*

On the other side of the road above the car park is the Time Ball Tower. This dates from 1894; its purpose was to act as an accurate reference for ships' navigators to set their clocks as the ball on the roof fell. Correct time was vital for the navigator to be able to determine precise longitude before the development of more modern equipment. Beside the tower is a 100-year-old **Dragon Tree** from the Canary Islands, and next to the tree is the original **Harbour Master's Residence**, 1860.

Two Oceans Aquarium
Dock Rd, **T** 021-4183823, www.aquarium.co.za *0930-1800. Daily feeds at 1530. R55, kids R25. Map 3, C9, p251 See also Kids, p215*

A top attraction on the Waterfront is this aquarium, focusing on the unique Cape marine environment created by the merging of the Atlantic and Indian Oceans. The display begins with a walk through the Indian Ocean, where visitors follow a route past tanks filled with a multitude of colourful fish, giant spider crabs and phosphorescent jellyfish, floating in a mesmerising circular current. Children are well catered for, with touch pools and the Alpha Activity Centre which hosts free puppet shows and face painting. The main wall here is part of the Diving Animals pool, where you can watch Cape fur seals dart and dive before the glass. The kelp forest tank is a highlight, an extraordinary tangle of giant kelp swaying drunkenly in artificial tides. Top draw is the predators exhibit, an enormous tank complete with glass tunnel, holding ragged-tooth sharks, eagle rays, turtles, and some impressively large hunting fish. There are daily feeds at 1530. It is possible to dive in the tank: certified divers can pay R400 to dive for half an hour. You must book a day in advance. It is a very safe but hair-raising experience, and thoroughly recommended for a first-time shark dive.

★ Robben Island

Tours are run by the Robben Island Museum, **T** 021-4134200, www.robben-island.org.za *0900-1800. R150 for adults, R70 for children under 17. Book a day ahead as tickets sell out. Boats leave on the hour between 0900 and 1500. Allow 3 hours. Map, inside back cover*

Lying 13 km off Green Point's shores, Robben Island is best known as the notorious prison that held many of the ANC's most prominent members, including **Nelson Mandela** and **Walter Sisulu.** It was originally named by the Dutch, after the term for seals, 'rob' – actually a misnomer as none are found here. The island's history of occupation started in 1806, when John Murray was granted permission by the British to conduct whaling from the island. During this period the authorities started to use the island as a dumping ground for common convicts; these were brought back to the mainland in 1843, and their accommodation was deemed suitable for lepers and the mentally ill. These were in turn moved to the mainland between 1913 and 1931, and the island entered a new era as a military base during the Second World War. In 1960 the military passed control of the island over to the Department of Prisons, and it remained a prison until 1996. In 1999 the island was declared a World Heritage Site by UNESCO.

Robben Island's effectiveness as a prison did not rest simply with the fact that escape was virtually impossible. The authorities anticipated that the idea of 'out of sight, out of

! All tour guides on Robben Island were once political prisoners here, offering an honest insight to prison life under apartheid.

A protective ring

Karamats are the tombs of Imams who lived and worked with the Muslim community of Cape Town. They are dotted around Cape Town in a circle that is believed to provide the city with a protective spiritual boundary, preventing natural disasters. Little is made of the Karamats in tourist literature, but for devout Cape Muslims they are very important. Before embarking upon *haj* a local muslim will visit each Karamat in turn. There is one on Robben Island. Others can be seen on the slopes of Signal Hill and in Constantia Valley.

mind' would be particularly applicable here, and to some extent they were right. Certainly, its isolation did much to break the spirit of political prisoners, not least **Robert Sobukwe**'s. Sobukwe was the leader of the Pan African Congress, and was kept in solitary confinement for nine years. Although other political prisoners were spared that horror, in 1971 they were separated from common law prisoners, as they were deemed a bad influence. Conditions were harsh, with forced hard labour and routine beatings. Much of the daily running of the maximum security prison was designed to reinforce racial divisions: all the warders, and none of the prisoners, were white; black prisoners, unlike those deemed coloured, had to wear short trousers and were given smaller food rations. Contact with the outside world was virtually non-existent – visitors had to apply for permission six months in advance and were allowed to stay for just half an hour. Newspapers were banned and letters were limited to one every six months. Yet despite these measures, the B-Section, which housed Mandela and other major political prisoners, became the international focus of the fight against apartheid. The last political prisoners left the island in 1991.

Tours begin with a drive around the key sites on the island, including Sobukwe's house, the lime quarry where Mandela was forced to work, the leper cemetery, and the houses of former warders. It is also possible to view wildlife – as a prison, the area was strictly protected, allowing the fish and bird populations to flourish. There are over 100 species of bird on the island, and it is an important breeding site for African penguins.

Atlantic Seaboard

*Stretching from Green Point to the Cape of Good Hope, this is the peninsula's most spectacular coastline, at times clinging dramatically to the **Twelve Apostles**, the spine of mountains stretching south. The area is best known for its beautiful beaches, including famous Clifton, the spot to mingle with the bronzed glitterati, from Cape Town socialites to supermodels.*

*Closest to the city are the less glamorous suburbs of **Green Point** and **Sea Point**, both lacking beaches and crammed with modern apartment blocks, but each with a different appeal. Green Point and the colourful Waterkant area is nightlife central and the main gay and lesbian hub, while Sea Point has more of a family seaside holiday feel. Further along are **Clifton** and **Camps Bay**, the latter offering a perfect arch of palm-fringed sand backed with pavement cafés and seafood restaurants. From here the rocky coast is surprisingly undeveloped, with just a handful of holiday homes backing onto surfing beaches, before the coastal road passes through **Hout Bay** with its beautiful rock promontories and working harbour, dishing up fresh fish and chips. The bay marks the beginning of **Chapman's Peak Drive**, perhaps the most spectacular stretch of road in South Africa.*

▸▸ *See Sleeping p109, Eating and drinking p138, Bars and clubs p165*

◉ Sights

Green Point and Sea Point
Map 3, p250 and Map 4, p252

Although these are the closest seaside areas to the city, they lack much of the charm and character found in the rest of Cape Town. Both are a mixture of high-rise apartment blocks lining the rocky seafront, and more attractive Victorian bungalows creeping up the slopes of Signal Hill. The Waterkant area of Green Point has become the focus of Cape Town's gay scene, with a great selection of fashionable cafés, quirky boutiques and late-night clubs. Sea Point has an excellent selection of accommodation, as well as a good range of shops and restaurants more geared towards families. The beach is unsafe for swimming, although there are a couple of rock pools, including Graaf's Pool (men only) and Milton's Pool.

★ Clifton Beach
Map 1, B2, p246

Cape Town's best-known beaches stretch along Clifton, and are renowned as the playground of the young and wealthy – expect well-groomed socialites mingling with the odd celebrity. Other than being hotspots of high society, Clifton's four sheltered beaches are stunning, small arches of powder-soft white sand sloping gently into turquoise water. The beaches are divided by rocky outcrops and are numbered: First, Second, Third and Fourth. Each has a distinct character – if you're bronzed and beautiful, head to First beach. More demure visitors will feel comfortable on Fourth, which is popular with families, while Third is the main gay beach, although perfect pecs are an essential accessory. The sunbathing and swimming are good on all the beaches, but note that the water is very cold – usually around 12 degrees. Most of the relatively small-scale development has been behind the beaches against the cliff face (some impressive houses can be glimpsed from the winding steps leading from the road). Be warned that there is limited parking and it's a steep climb down footpaths to the beach.

Camps Bay
Map 5, p253

Following the coast south, you soon skirt around a hill and come out over Camps Bay, a long arch of sand backed by the Twelve Apostles. This is one of the most beautiful (and most photographed) beaches in the world, but the calm cobalt water belies its chilliness. The sand is also less sheltered than at Clifton, and sunbathing here on a windy day can be quite painful. But there are other distractions; the beachfront is lined with a number of excellent seafood restaurants, and having a sundowner followed by a superb meal is the perfect ending to a day in Cape Town.

The stunning drive between Camps Bay and Hout Bay winds between the sea and the wild slopes of the Twelve Apostles. Apart from the turning to **Llandudno**, there is no easy access to the coast until you reach Hout Bay. Llandudno itself is a small, exclusive settlement with a fine beach and excellent surf.

Hout Bay
Map 1, E1, p246

Hout Bay may seem strangely familiar – little surprise considering how often it is featured on postcards and coffee table books. It is a perfect cove with a white sandy beach, clear blue waters and a busy fishing harbour. The famous Chapman's Peak Drive begins from here, and as the sun sets in the summer months every pullover along the road gets occupied by groups watching the sun go down with a drink in hand.

Before Cape Town had established itself as the foremost port in the area, Hout Bay was an important naturally sheltered anchorage. Today, activity centres around two locations: at the western end of the bay is the fishing harbour; at the other end is a collection of shops and popular restaurants. By the harbour is a commercial complex known as **Mariners Wharf**, the first of its kind in South Africa and a very popular attraction. It is based upon Fisherman's Wharf in San Francisco, with a string of fish 'n' chips restaurants, souvenir shops, boats for hire as well as a fish market known as **Snoekies Fresh Fish Market**, close to the harbour gates.

Drumbeat Charters, T 021-7914441, and **Nauticat**, T 021-7907278, www.nauticatcharters.co.za, conduct tours to see seals on **Duiker Island** in season (August to April). Trips depart roughly every hour until 1500 and cost R45 for an hour's trip. They are a good opportunity to admire the Cape peninsula from the sea.

World of Birds, at Valley Road, is set in 4 km of open land with over 400 species of birds in a series of walk-through averies. There's also the Monkey Jungle, populated with squirrel monkeys. T 021-7902730, www.worldofbirds.org.za, *daily 0900-1700*.

★ Chapman's Peak Drive
Map 1, E2, p246

It is worth hiring a car for a day just to drive along Chapman's Peak Drive, a breathtaking 15-km route carved into the cliffs 600 m above the sea. The route was recently re-opened following extensive repairs and the rigging up of giant nets to catch falling rocks. It's now a toll road, costing R20 per car. The views of the coast and ocean are outstanding and one of the Cape's highlights. The best time to drive along here is close to sunset in the summer, but the views of Hout Bay on one side, and Noordhoek beach on the other, are recommended at any time.

★ **Beaches**

Best

- •Clifton, p54
- •Llandudno, p55
- •Noordhoek, p57
- •Muizenberg, p67
- •Boulders Beach, p73

Cape Town

Noordhoek
Map 1, F2, p246

The greatest attraction here is the 8-km long deserted beach with a couple of tidal lagoons behind it which offer excellent bird watching. The Red Herring Trading Post on Beach Road is a good shopping spot, including a Kakapo farm stall and bakery, Milkwood Craft Co-op, curios and clothes. This is also a popular setting for horse riding along the shore. Contact **Nordhoek Beach Horse Rides**, **T** 082-7741191 (cell), www.horseriding.co.za, or **Sleepy Hollow Horse Riding**, **T** 021-7892341.

Kommetjie
Map 1, G1, p247

Driving along the Atlantic side of the peninsula, you could miss Kommetjie altogether if you were to follow the signs for Ocean View. The settlement is small with a pub, restaurant, caravan park and little else. It is, however, a major surfing spot and Long Beach to the north is always busy with surfers, even in winter. There is also an interesting walk along Long Beach to the wreck of the *Kakapo*, a steamship which was beached here in May 1900 on her maiden voyage when the captain apparently mistook Chapman's Peak for Cape Point during a storm.

★ Cape of Good Hope Nature Reserve

T 021-7018692, www.cpnp.co.za   *0600-1800 Oct-Mar, 0700-1700 Apr-Sep. R35. Visiting in your own vehicle is recommended (65 km from the centre). Several companies also organize good day trips.   Map 1, K3, p247   See also Boat tours, p25*

The Cape of Good Hope Nature Reserve, now part of the **Table Mountain National Park**, is one of the peninsula's highlights, a dramatically wild area of towering cliffs, excellent hiking and deserted beaches, straddling the ground between the Atlantic Seaboard and False Bay. The reserve was established in 1939 to protect the unique flora and fauna of this stretch of coast. It is an integral part of the **Cape Floristic Kingdom**, the smallest but richest of the world's six floral kingdoms. A frequently quoted statistic is that within the 7,750 ha of the reserve there are as many different plant species as there are in the whole of the British Isles. In addition to this there are several different species of antelope: eland, bontebok, springbok, Cape grysbok, red hartebeest and grey rhebok, as well as the elusive Cape mountain zebra, snakes, tortoises and pesky baboons. Needless to say, it's a popular place to visit. If possible, avoid going at the weekend or during school holidays.

Although the strong winds and the low lying vegetation are not ideal for birds, over 250 species have been recorded here, of which about 100 are known to breed within the reserve. There are plenty of vantage points where you can watch sea birds such as the Cape gannet, shy albatross, sooty shearwater, Sabine's gull and Cory's shearwater. In the strandveld vegetation along the coast you can expect to see fruit-eating birds such as the Cape robin and bully canary. Some rarities found here include the white-rumped sandpiper from South America, macaroni penguins from Antarctica and the purple gallinule from the US.

Cape Point Lighthouse is nothing special in itself, but the climb up here is well worth it for the best views of Cape Point. On a clear day the ocean views stretching all around are incredible – as is the wind, so be sure to hold on to hats and sunglasses. You can take the funicular to the top, but the 20-minute walk allows better views of the coast. If you have a good head for heights, there is a spectacular walk to the modern lighthouse at Diaz Point. From the renovated old lighthouse you can see the path running along the left side of the narrow cliff that makes up the point. The round trip takes about 30 minutes. Do not attempt it if it is windy – the winds around the Cape can reach up to 55 knots (100 km per hour). As you look down from the lighthouse at Cape Point it is easy to see how ships could suffer on a dark night in a storm, especially before the lighthouse was built. There are 23 wrecks in the waters around the Cape, five of which can be seen when walking in the reserve. The first boat to be wrecked here was the *Flying Dutchman* in 1680, which has since become famous as a ghost ship. Legend has it that the boat is cursed to sail around the Cape of Good Hope forever and can be sighted during a storm. The most famous sighting was by midshipman King George V in 1881.

⬤ *There are several marked hiking paths and maps are available from the information office at the top of the funicular. One of the most spectacular walks is along the coast from Rooikrans towards Buffels Bay. Look out for the wreck, The Tania, from 1972.*

Southern Suburbs

Hugging the lower slopes of Table Mountain and stretching southeast away from the city centre, towards Constantia and False Bay, are Cape Town's Southern Suburbs. These encompass the bulk of Cape Town's suburban sprawl, once the enclave of largely affluent whites but today an interesting mix of areas with a number of attractions. The suburbs start with the rundown, working-class area of **Woodstock** *just outside the City Bowl on the slopes of* **Devil's Peak**, *and continue all the way around the mountain, finishing just before* **False Bay** *in the beautiful wine- growing area of* **Constantia** *with*

*its manicured gardens, forests and fortified mansions. Behind the mountain, rolling away from the mountain's slopes, are the **Cape Flats**, a vast sprawl of coloured and black townships and mushrooming shanty towns, home to the majority of Cape Town's residents but rarely visited by tourists. The main draw in the Southern Suburbs are the magnificent **Kirstenbosch Botanical Gardens** and Constantia's historical vineyards and elegant hotels, but there are a number of more unconventional attractions – like bar-hopping in **Observatory**, watching a rugby match at **Newlands** or shopping in one of Cape Town's glitziest malls.*

▸▸ *See Sleeping p115, Eating and drinking p142, Bars and clubs p168*

A hire car is the best way to tour the suburbs. Although the Metro service between the city centre and Simon's Town runs through all the suburbs, it is best avoided at times other than rush hour.

 Sights

Woodstock and Observatory
Map 6 and 7, p253 and 254

The first suburb, **Woodstock**, is a mixed commercial and residential area, historically a working-class coloured district. In the 19th century it was a thriving community, when it was known as Papendorp. It became a municipality in 1881 and the local residents were invited to choose a new name. The most popular drinking haunt at the time was the *Woodstock Hotel*, and so the suburb got its present name. Today it is rundown and rather depressing, although the back streets are an attractive mesh of Victorian bungalows. Avoid driving along Main Road here after dark.

Observatory is an offbeat suburb of tightly packed Victorian houses, narrow streets and student hangouts. It is known as something of a bohemian enclave, and once settled here you can

quickly forget about the town centre or Waterfront. Being close to
the university, there is a wide range of trendy bars, cafés and
restaurants catering for a mixed scene of students, hippie types
and budget backpackers. This is a good area to stay in and has an
enjoyably liberal atmosphere not so easily found in some of the
other suburbs. The observatory after which the suburb is named is
where Station Road intersects Liesbeeck Parkway. Aside from
making astronomical observations the observatory was
responsible for accurate standard time in South Africa. It has also
been an important meteorological centre and has a seismograph
which records earthquakes around the world. Observatory is also
where you'll find the Groot Schuur Hospital on Main Road, the site
of the world's first heart transplant.

Mowbray, Rosebank and Rondebosch
Map 1, C4, p246

The next suburbs of Mowbray, Rosebank and Rondebosch lie just
below the University of Cape Town. Again, they are popular with
students and have a good selection of restaurants and shops.
Early written accounts describe the area as wild country, with the
farmers frequently losing livestock to hyenas, lions and leopards –
an image that is hard to imagine as you sit in the evening rush
hour traffic jam on Rhodes Drive. In Rondebosch is Groot Schuur,
the Prime Minister's official residence and Westbrooke, home of
the State President.

   A lesser-known but fascinating tourist attraction in the area is
the **Irma Stern Museum** (Cecil Rd, Rosebank, **T** 021-6855686,
Tue-Sat 1000-1700, R10). Irma Stern was one of South Africa's
pioneering artists and her lovely house, on Cecil Road, displays a
mixture of her own works, a collection of artefacts from across
Africa, and some fine pieces of antique furniture from overseas –
17th-century Spanish chairs, 19th-century German oak furniture
and Swiss *mardi gras* masks. Her portraits are particularly poignant

and those of her close friends are superb, while her religious art is rather more disturbing. Stern's studio, complete with paint brushes and palettes, has been left as it was when she died. The most important African items were collected in the Congo and Zanzibar. Of particular note is the Buli Stool, one of only 20 known carvings by a master carver from southeast Zaire.

The best-known attraction in the area is the **Rhodes Memorial**, off Rhodes Drive, by the Rondebosch turning (**T** 021-6899151, Nov-April 0730-1900, May-Oct 0800-1800). The imposing granite memorial to Cecil John Rhodes (Cape Prime Minister from 1890-96) was designed by Francis Masey and Sir Herbert Baker. Four bronze lions flank a wide flight of steps which lead up to a Greek temple. The temple houses an immense bronze head of Rhodes, wrought by JM Swan. Above the head are the words "slave to the spirit and life work of Cecil John Rhodes who loved and served South Africa". At the base of the steps is an immense bronze mounted figure of Physical Energy given to South Africa by GF Watts, a well-regarded sculptor of the time; the original stands in Hyde Park, London. Other than the memorial, the great attraction here is the magnificent view of the Cape Flats and the Southern Suburbs. Behind the memorial are a number of popular trails leading up the slopes of Devil's Peak.

● *Tucked away here is an excellent little tea house set in a garden of blue hydrangeas which serves good cheesecake, sandwiches and cream teas – a popular spot, especially for lunch at weekends.*

South of Rondebosch
Map 1, C4/D4, p246

By this point the Southern Suburbs have reached right around Devil's Peak and the shadowy peaks dominating the views present an unfamiliar view of Table Mountain. **Newlands** backs right up to the slopes of the mountain and is probably best known for being the home to Western Province Rugby Union and the beautiful

Newlands cricket test ground. Sports fans shouldn't miss the chance of seeing a game here. There are several good hotels and guesthouses in the area. Also in Newlands is the **Rugby Museum**, on Boundary Road, housed in the Sports Medical Research Institute Building, (**T** 021-6596700, Mon-Fri 0830-1700, free). The collection commemorates the history of the sport in the country and is also home to the **Currie Cup**, which is the premier domestic competition trophy.

Claremont offers little of interest other than the upmarket Cavendish Square Complex on Main Rd, and the nearby **Ardene Gardens**. This is a Victorian park which was first planted in 1845 by Ralph Arderne, who was so charmed by the Cape while en route for Australia that he decided to settle here instead. He succeeded in creating a garden that would represent the flora of the world. Today the arboretum with specimens from all over the world is one of the best collection of trees in South Africa. The gardens were declared a historical monument in 1962.

A little further along the main road takes you to **Wynberg**. Apart from a few curio shops, the main attraction here is the district known as **Little Chelsea**, a group of well-preserved 19th-century homes.

★ Kirstenbosch Botanical Gardens

T 021-7998800, www.nbi.ac.za *Sep-Mar 0800-1900, Apr-Aug 0800-1800. R20. The easiest way of getting here is by hire car. There is a Golden Arrow bus service from Adderley St from Mon-Fri, but these tend to be slow. Alternatively, take a Rikki taxi or an organized city tour which includes Kirstenbosch in its itinerary. Map 1, D3, p246*

Kirstenbosch are South Africa's oldest, largest and most exquisite botanical gardens. They are among the finest in the world, their setting alone incomparable. The gardens stretch up the eastern slopes of Table Mountain, merging seamlessly with the *fynbos* of the steep drops above. Cecil Rhodes bought Kirstenbosch farm in

★ **Markets**

Best
- The Pan-African Market, Long Street, p192
- Greenmarket Square, p195
- Church Street Market, p195
- Grand Parade Market, p195
- Green Point Market, p196

1895 and promptly presented the site to the people of South Africa with the intention that it become a botanical garden. The most enjoyable way of experiencing the gardens today is at one of the **Sunset Concerts** held on Sundays in summer, where visitors bring picnics and lounge before a makeshift stage listening to live jazz, classical concerts and world music.

As with all botanical gardens they are divided into smaller specialist gardens. Highlights include the Fragrance garden, the Dell, the Medicinal Plants garden and Van Riebeeck's Hedge.

The **Fragrance garden** features herbs and flowers set out to make the most of their scents. On a warm day, when volatile oils are released by the plants, there are some rather overpowering aromas. **The Dell** follows a beautifully shaded path snaking beneath ferns and along a stream. Indigenous South African herbs can be inspected in the **Medicinal Plants** garden, each one identified and used by the Khoi and San peoples in the treatment of a variety of ailments. The plants' uses are identified on plaques, and it seems that most ailments are covered – from kidney trouble and rheumatics to coughs and piles. For a sense of the past, it is worth visiting what is known as **Van Riebeeck's Hedge**. Back in 1660 a hedge of wild almond trees was planted by Van Riebeeck as part of a physical boundary to try and prevent cattle rustling. Segments still remain today within the garden. The **Skeleton Path** can be followed all the way to the summit of

Top table
Flat-topped Table Mountain is the symbol of the city and dominates the skyline.

1 *The 19th-century Clock Tower on the Victoria and Alfred Waterfront is today juxtaposed by the ultra-modern Nelson Mandela Gateway to Robben Island.* ▶▶ *See page 48.*

2 *Music permeates the life and soul of the city, whether it's buskers entertaining the crowds in the city centre or the greats of Cape Jazz performing at the prestigious North Sea Jazz Festival.* ▶▶ *See page 178.*

3 *In 1834 the declaration to free all slaves was made from Greenmarket Square. Today the square is a popular meeting place, with a busy daily market.* ▶▶ *See pages 45 and 195.*

4 *The eastern slopes of Table Mountain provide a magical setting for the Kirstenbosch Botanical Gardens, founded by Cecil Rhodes in 1895.* ▶▶ *See page 63.*

5 *Camps Bay has a wide arc of sandy beach, backed by restaurants and cafés that are popular with Cape Town's glitterati.* ▶▶ *See page 55.*

6 *Cruise along Chapman's Peak Drive, a breathtaking 15-km route carved into the cliffs 600 m above the sea.* ▶▶ *See page 56.*

Cape candy
Brightly painted houses and cobbled streets are a distinctive feature of the Bo-Kaap, Cape Town's characterful Islamic district.

Table Mountain. It starts off as a stepped path, but becomes fairly steep near the top. It involves a climb up a rocky waterfall – take special care in the wet season.

● *The café serves over-priced sandwiches and cakes – better value and with far nicer views is the restaurant inside the gardens, just around the corner from the entrance (open until 2200). Another alternative is the picnic hamper service.*

Constantia
Map 1, D3, p246

South of the Botanical Gardens lies Cape Town's most elegant suburb, the verdant area of Constantia and its wine estates. This historical district was the first site of wine-making in South Africa, and today it is an attractive introduction to the country's wine heritage, as well as offering some fine examples of Cape Dutch architecture.

There are five estates here, of which **Groot Constantia**, **T** 021-7945128, www.grootconstantia.co.za, is the best known and definitely worth a visit. **Buitenverwatchting**, **T** 021- 7945190, www.buitenverwachting.co.za, is a working estate with an excellent restaurant. **Klein Constantia**, **T** 021-7945188, is a beautifully hilly estate with a great tasting centre, and is famed for its dessert wine, Vin de Constance, allegedly Napoleon's favourite wine. **Constantia Uitsig**, **T** 021-7941810, www.constantiauitsig.co.za, has fine wines, luxury accommodation and two superb restaurants, *Constantia Uitsig* and *La Colombe*. **Steenberg**, **T** 021-7132222, www.steenberghotel.com, also offers superb wines, as well as luxurious lodgings, a good restaurant and a golf course.

The best-known wine estate, **Groot Constantia**, has some of the finest Cape Dutch architecture in South Africa, and with its rolling vineyard setting and wine-tasting centre is a delightful place to spend a few hours – although it does get correspondingly swamped with tour buses in high season. The main house was originally home to Cape Governor Simon van der Stel between 1699 and 1712. He named the estate after Constantia, the daughter of the company official who had granted the land to him. Before his death, van der Stel planted most of the vines, but it was not until 1778 that the estate became famous for its wines. The magnificent wine cellar behind the main house was designed by the renowned French architect, Louis Thibault. The main house is now a museum filled with period furniture, *open 0900-1700/1800, R10*. There are two restaurants on site: *Jonkershuis* has traditional Cape food; *Simon's* serves burgers, salads and seafood. Wine tastings take place at the sales centre just to the right of the main entrance, and cost R20 for five wines; cheese platters are also available. Cellar tours run every hour on the hour.

False Bay

*On the other side of the peninsula lies False Bay, characterized by a string of seaside resorts that have a very different feel from the Atlantic Seaboard. Here the main emphasis is on family holidays, and **Muizenberg**, **Simon's Town** and **Kalk Bay** have neither the frenetic pace nor the spectacular landscape of the Atlantic Seaboard. This can mean that they can seem rather twee compared to the slick pace of Cape Town's major haunts, but they also offer excellent beaches and are more laid back – although the towns are far from quiet during peak season. The main attraction here is the warm water; temperatures can be as much as 8°C higher than at Camps Bay or Clifton. While Muizenberg has the finest beach and Simon's Town the best facilities, Kalk Bay is the most enjoyable spot, busy with cafés and antique shops and with a tiny working harbour selling fresh fish straight off the boats. In spring there is the added advantage of seeing calving **whales** in False Bay, with good numbers of Southern Right, humpback and bryde whales.*

▸▸ *See Sleeping p118, Eating and drinking p145*

The Metro train line continues through the southern suburbs to Simon's Town – the stretch following False Bay is spectacular. Trains leave approximately every 30 mins, with the last trains leaving Simon's Town at around 2000, but check the train information line for up-to-date times: T 080121211. There have been reports of crime on the trains, so avoid them at times other than rush hour. There are two road routes across the mountainous spine linking the roads which hug the coast around the peninsula, but the most scenic route is the M65 along the coast from the Atlantic Seaboard to False Bay.

Sights

Muizenberg
Map 1, F4, p246

Travelling out from the city centre, this is the first settlement you reach on False Bay. Muizenberg was first propelled to the forefront of popularity when **Cecil Rhodes** bought a cottage here in 1899. Many other wealthy people followed, building some fine Victorian and Edwardian cottages along the back streets, and attracting the likes of Agatha Christie and Rudyard Kipling to its shores.

Sadly, today the town and its seafront have become rundown and tatty, although there have been murmurings of a soon-to-be-planned face lift. Nevertheless, the beach itself remains beautiful: a vast stretch of powdery white sand sloping gently to the water. It is safe for swimming as there is no backwash, and it is easy for surfers. **Sunrise Beach**, 2 km to the east, is the most popular spot today. Behind **West Beach** is a large red and white striped pavilion built in the 1970s, a fun fair, mini golf, fast food outlets, and a collection of distinctive, colourful private bathing huts, reproductions of those that were built here in the 19th century.

The walk along the main street towards St James is known locally as the **Historic Mile** and takes you past a number of interesting historic buildings. Some of these are national monuments, but most are closed to the public. The first building of note is the **Station building**, a fine example of art deco architecture built in 1912. On the other side of the road is **Het Post Huijs**, thought to be the oldest building in False Bay, dating back to 1673. A few doors down is the grand Italian mansion that until recently held the **Natale Labia Museum**. This was part of the National Gallery but was closed at time of writing and looks unlikely to reopen. The house was built in 1929 as the official residence for Italy's diplomatic representative to South Africa, Prince Natale Labia. **Rhodes Cottage**, at number 246, is surprisingly small and austere for someone as wealthy as Cecil Rhodes. It has been restored and now contains many of his personal items and displays on his life and achievements.

There are several paths leading from the back of the town into the Kalk Bay Mountains and the Silvermine Nature Reserve.

St James
Map 1, G3, p247

Just beyond Muizenberg lies the more upmarket resort of St James, an appealing village with characteristic brightly coloured bathing huts lined along its shore. The village is named after a Roman Catholic Church which was built here in 1854 to save Catholics having to travel as far as Simon's Town to attend services – interestingly, some of the early settlers were Catholic Filipino fishermen. There is a small sheltered beach and reasonable surf off Danger Beach. St James is a suitable starting point for a hike in the excellent **Silvermine Nature Reserve**. A path starts on Boyes Drive and climbs up through the Spes Bona Forest to Tartarus Cave. The views alone are worth the hike (see p70 for further details).

Kalk Bay
Map 1, G3, p247

Kalk Bay is one of the most attractive settlements on False Bay with a bustling fish harbour and a bohemian vibe making it a great spot to relax for a day or two. The town is named after the lime kilns which produced *kalk* from shells in the 17th century. An important local product, the lime created the white-walled appearance of many new houses in the Cape, especially amongst the Bo-Kaap community. Until the arrival of the railway in 1883, the local fishermen hunted whales, seals and small fish. Today it remains a fishing harbour, worked mainly by a coloured community which somehow escaped the Group Areas Act under apartheid. It is one of the few remaining coloured settlements on the peninsula.

Main Road is an appealing spot, lined with antique shops and art galleries, and the beach is sandy and safe for swimming, with a couple of tidal pools for children to explore. Between June and July the harbour is busy with the season for snoek, one of the most plentiful local fish harvests. Look out for the returning deep sea fishing boats around the middle of the day, as there's a daily impromptu quayside auction. You can buy a variety of fresh fish at the counters and for an extra R3 get them to gut them for you too. Another attraction is **Seal Island**, an important breeding ground for birds and seals, the latter attracting hungry great white sharks. Cruises run from Simon's Town. You should also look out for the **Holy Trinity Church** on the Main Road. It has a thatched roof, but its appeal is the windows, considered to be some of the finest in the Cape. On Quarterdeck Road is a tiny mosque built in the 1800s.

High up behind the town is **Boyes Drive**, a scenic route connecting the bay with Muizenburg. It's a spectacular route offering sweeping views of False Bay and the Atlantic, and takes just ten minute to complete – look out for the signs from Main Road as you head out of Kalk Bay towards Simon's Town.

Clovelly
Map 1, G3, p247

Continuing along the main road, the next settlement you reach is Clovelly, tucked between the waters of False Bay and the mountains of the Silvermine Reserve. Along the main street are several shops and places to have a snack. Visitors from the west country in Britain might be interested to know that this community is named after the village in Devon. Golf enthusiasts should head a little way inland for the *Clovelly Country Club*. To use the golf course (18 holes) or eat in the restaurant you need to take out temporary membership.

Silvermine Nature Reserve
Access into the reserve is between sunrise and sunset, see over page for getting there details; 1 Sep-31 Mar, 0800-1900; 1 Apr-31 Aug, 0800-1800. Map 1, F3, p246

This is a popular local reserve, now part of the **Table Mountain National Park**, but it is not often visited by overseas visitors. Table Mountain and Cape Point tend to dominate the open-air attractions, and rightly so, but the Silvermine Nature Reserve is also well worth a visit if you enjoy hiking, and are hankering after tremendous views across False Bay and the Atlantic Ocean from the high peaks.

Like much of the Cape, the reserve encompasses one of the oldest floral kingdoms in the world. Over 900 rare and endangered species have been recorded in the mountains. In addition to the plants there are a couple of patches of indigenous forest in the Spes Bona and Echo valleys. Ornithologists should look out for black eagles, ground woodpeckers, orange-breasted sunbirds and rock kestrels. If you're extremely lucky, you may also come across small shy mammals such as lynx, porcupine and various species of mongoose.

The reserve is split into two sections by the Ou Kaapseweg Road as it crosses the Kalk Bay Mountains – the eastern sector and western sector. There is no public transport along this road. By car you can either approach from the Cape Town side or from Noordhoek and Fish Hoek. A variety of footpaths from Muizenberg, St James and Kalk Bay lead into the reserve and make a pleasant day trip from Cape Town.

Fish Hoek
Map 1, G3, p247

Fish Hoek is one of the most conservative settlements on the coast, not least as the sale of alcohol is prohibited here. It does, however, have a fine beach, perhaps the best for swimming after Muizenberg. From mid-August, there is a good chance of catching a glimpse of whales from here. The next resort is tiny Glencairn, which has one of the best mid-range hotels on False Bay (see Sleeping p101).

Peers Cave, inland from the Country Club, is a well-known rock shelter where six fossilized human skeletons were discovered in 1927, dated at over 10,000 years old. There are also some paintings on the walls, and it is now a national monument. From the police station it is about 45 minutes' walk to the cave, crossing ancient sand dunes which are evidence of changes in sea level.

Simon's Town
Map 1, I3, p247

This is the prettiest town on False Bay, with a pleasant atmosphere and numerous Victorian buildings lining the main road. The town is fairly quiet for most of the year but becomes very busy with families during the summer school holidays. Whenever you visit, take some time to wander up the hill away from the main road – the quiet, bougainvillea-bedecked houses and cobbled streets with their sea views are a lovely retreat from the busy beaches.

The main swimming spot is **Seaforth Beach**, not far from Boulders Beach (see below). To get there, turn off St George's Road into Seaforth Road after passing the navy block to the left. The beach is the second on the right, on Kleintuin Road. A little further towards Cape Point are two other popular bathing beaches, **Windmill** and **Fisherman's**. The swimming is safe, but there is no surf due to offshore rocks which protect the beach. Look out for some giant pots, a legacy from whaling days, when they were used for melting whale blubber.

Diving is a very popular activity around the Cape Peninsula. See Sports, p204 for outfits. There is a 9-hole, 18-tee, links course on the seafront, just by the turning for Boulders Beach. This is a narrow course and is a real test for anyone not used to playing in very windy conditions. See Sports, p201.

Just before you hit the centre of town is the **Simon's Town Museum**, (**T** 021-7863046, Mon-Fri 0900-1600, Sat 1000-1300, Sun 1100-1300, donation), with displays on its history as a naval base for the British and South African navies. The museum organizes a guided walk along the 'Historical Mile' on Tue and Sat, R20. Nearby, the **South Africa Naval Museum**, (**T** 021-7874686, daily 1000-1600, donation) includes a collection of model ships, a modern submarine control room plus relics from the Martello Tower. In the centre of town, the **Quayside Centre** is a smart development on Wharf Street, next to Jubilee Square, which has greatly enhanced the seafront. Cruises to Cape Point can be booked here.

Round the corner from Jubilee Square, and worth a quick peek, is the **Warrior Toy Museum** (daily 1000-1600, R3), a tiny museum with an impressive collection of model cars, trains, dolls and toy soldiers. The nearby **Heritage** Museum (**T** 021-7862302, Tue-Fri, 1100-1600, R3), faithfully charts the history of the Muslim community in Simon's Town. The town was designated a 'white' area during the Group Area Act and over 7,000 people classified as coloured were relocated. The exhibition in Heritage House consists mainly of pictures and artefacts dating back to the turn of the century.

A number of boat trips to the Cape of Good Hope originate from Simon's Town harbour. Taking a trip from here allows views of the spectacular coastline and its hinterland from a different angle. In addition to straightforward sightseeing tours, there are several options for viewing bird life, seals and whales during the right season. See Boat operators, p25.

Whale watching season starts in October. Rules surrounding trips to see the whales are very stringent, and only one boat a year is given a permit to run cruises. These change every year, so it is best to contact the very helpful and informative **Publicity Association**, **T** 021-7862436, www.simonstown.com.

★ Boulders Beach
T 021-7862329, boulders@parks-sa.co.za *0800-1700. R15.*
Map 1, I3, p247

About 2 km south of Simon's Town is Boulders Beach, a lovely series of sandy coves surrounded by huge boulders (hence the name). It is a peaceful spot, safe for swimming and gently shelving, making it good for children. The real attraction, though, is the colony of African penguins that live and nest between the boulders. Boulders Coastal Park has been created to protect the little creatures, and their numbers have flourished. Bizarrely, they take little notice of their sunbathing neighbours and happily go about their business of swimming, waddling and braying (their characteristic braying was the reason they were, until recently, known as Jackass penguins). The best time to see large numbers is just before sunset, when they return from a day's feeding at sea. The admission charge is well worth it to get close to the penguins, but avoid the nesting areas. The first cove gets very busy with families at weekends and during school holidays. Walk along the boardwalk or crawl under the rocks on one side of the beach to get to a more peaceful spot.

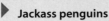

▶ Jackass penguins

This flightless sea bird is only found on the coast of southern Africa. Once they nested in guano burrows, today concrete piping can provide the necessary shelter. In the 1930s estimates put their population at over one million birds, but today less than 110,000 penguins are left. This considerable decline in the population has been put down to commercial fishing competing with their food stocks, and the collection of their eggs for food. They eat sardines, maasbanker, anchovy and squid. Boulders Beach and Betty's Bay, further along the coast, are the only places where they can be seen nesting on the mainland. These are some of the smaller penguins, but you won't get a better view unless you go to Antarctica or the Falkland Islands.

This is the last easy access to the sea on this side of the peninsula. Beyond Partridge Point the main road cuts into the hillside, and access to the beach is via steep footpaths. **Miller's Point** has a large caravan site plus a picnic area and a restaurant. The road climbs above the sea before rounding the mountains by Smitswinkel Bay. On a clear day you can look back to a perfect view of the cliffs plunging into the sea. A short distance from the shore is the Cape of Good Hope Nature Reserve entrance.

Rondevlei Nature Reserve
T 021-7062404, www.rondevlei.co.za *0730-1700/1900. R5. From Cape Town take the M5, and follow signs at Victoria Rd. Map 1, E4, p246*

Despite being surrounded by suburban sprawl this sanctuary is one of the best bird-watching spots close to Cape Town. The 120-km reserve was originally established to protect the birdlife and the

Hiking areas

coastal *fynbos*. There is a path which follows the swamp's edge, along which there are two lookout towers equipped with telescopes. There are several hides along the water's edge, and cuts within the reeds allow views across the water. As well as around 200 bird species, there is a small population of hippopotamus.

Tokai Forest

T 021-7127471. *Daily during daylight hours, donation. Take the M3 out of town towards the Southern Suburbs. Before Muizenberg, turn right into Tokai Street and follow the signs for Tokai Manor House. Map 1, E3, p246*

Tokai was set up as a forest nursery in 1883 to try and stem the destruction of forest reserves, and start a programme of conservation and reforestation. It is within the lands of an old wine estate, Tokai Homestead (1795), named after a wine region of Hungary. This is one of the few areas where the region's indigenous forest and some wildlife have been fully protected and preserved. The arboretum contains 40 tree species – there are two walking trails in the forest, and horse riding and mountain biking are possible in the low-lying section of the forest (permits from the main gate). One of the designated walks is marked by white 'elephants', a trail which leads you up the mountain through the forest to Elephant's Eye cave.

Museums and galleries

- **Bertram House** A Georgian house decorated with 19th-century British furnishings, p35.
- **Bo-Kaap Museum** Museum dedicated to Cape Malays, p47.
- **Castle of Good Hope** Home to three museums: William Fehr Collection, Secunde's House and a military museum, p41.
- **District Six Museum** Powerful and moving exhibitions giving a fascinating insight into apartheid, p42.
- **Gold of Africa Museum** A slick presentation of the history of gold mining, p45.
- **Heritage Museum** An excellent museum that charts the history of the Muslim community in Simon's Town, p72.
- **Holocaust Centre** This museum shockingly and intelligently examines the Holocaust, p36.
- **Irma Stern Museum** Displays of the artist's work, p61.
- **Jewish Museum** A rich and rare collection of items depicting the history of the Jewish community on the Cape, p35.
- **Koopmans-De Wet House** A restored house offering an interesting insight into the lives of cultured society in early 19th-century Cape Town, p44.
- **National Gallery** Houses local and international art, p37.
- **Rust en Vreugd** A restored 18th-century mansion with six galleries of art depicting the history of the Cape, p37.
- **Slave Church Museum** The oldest mission church in Cape Town now has a permanent display of the work throughout the Cape, p46.
- **Slave Lodge** This former lodge for slaves surprisingly celebrates colonialism although there are plans afoot to change the emphasis towards the slave trade, p39.
- **South Africa Museum and Planetarium** The city's most established museum specializes in natural history, ethnography and archaeology, p34.

The Whale Coast 79 The Whale Coast, a couple of hours' drive from Cape Town, lives up to its title from July to November, when large numbers of whales seek out the sheltered bays along the coast for breeding. Hermanus, a well-developed and pleasant seaside resort, is the most popular spot, but whales can be seen all along Walker Bay.

The Winelands 85 The Winelands is South Africa's oldest and most beautiful wine-producing area, a fertile series of valleys quite unlike the rest of the Western Cape. It is the Cape's biggest attraction after Cape Town, and its appeal is simple: it offers the chance to sample several hundred different wines in a historical and superbly scenic setting.

The Whale Coast

*Highlight of the evocatively named Whale Coast is **Hermanus**, which is best approached on the dramatic route from Gordon's Bay, where the mountains plunge straight into the ocean forming a coastline of steep cliffs, sandy coves and dangerous headlands. Elsewhere along the coast there are miles of sandy beaches, wrecks to scuba dive, the chance of seeing the great white shark, and the southernmost point in Africa – **Cape Agulhas**.*

▸▸ *See Sleeping p120 and Eating and drinking p148*

The easiest way to visit Hermanus and the Whale Coast is by car, but there are also regular mainline bus routes, and the Baz Bus goes from Cape Town to the Bot River Hotel, near Hermanus.

 Sights

Hermanus
120 km from Cape Town (via N2)

Hermanus has grown from a rustic fishing village to a much-visited tourist resort famed for its superb whale watching. It trumpets itself as having the world's best land-based whale watching, and indeed Walker Bay is host to impressive numbers during calving season (July to November). However, don't expect any private viewings – Hermanus is very popular and has a steady flow of binocular-wielding visitors throughout the year. While this means it can get very busy, there is also a good range of accommodation and restaurants, making it a great base for exploring the quieter

! Look out for the Hermanus Whale Crier, who wanders along the coast blowing a giant kelp horn to alert visitors to where the whales are. He is allegedly the only such crier in the world.

reaches of the coast. Alternatively, Hermanus is only a few hours from Cape Town, making it an easy day trip from the city.

The best way of seeing whales is by following the **Cliff Path** along the coast. It starts at the new harbour in Westcliff and follows the shore all the way round Walker Bay to Grotto Beach, a distance of just over 15 km. Between cliffs the path goes through stands of milkwood trees and takes you around the sandy beaches.

The **old harbour**, in the centre of town, is a national monument and is reached by a ramp leading down the cliffs from Market Square. There is an old jetty, a group of restored fishermen's cottages and the town museum, with displays based on the local fishing industry. The most interesting feature is the recorded sound of calls between whales. There is also a telescope to watch the whales further out. Outside the museum on the harbour ramp is a collection of small restored fishing boats, the earliest dating from 1855. Also on show are the drying racks for small fish and cement tables which were once used for gutting fish. (Mon-Sat 0900-1300, 1400-1700, Sun 1200-1600). The **new harbour**, to the west, is still a busy fishing port.

There are some good beaches just a short distance in either direction from the town centre. The best beaches to the west are found at Onrus and Vermont. **Grotto Beach** is the largest, best developed and most popular for swimming, and is one of just three Blue Flag beaches in South Africa. The fine white sands stretch beyond the Klein River Lagoon, and there are changing facilities, a restaurant and a beach shop. Slightly closer to the town centre is **Voëlklip Beach**, a little rundown, but with well-kept lawns behind the sand. Conditions are good for swimming and surfing. The most popular spot for surfers is **Kammabaai** next door to Voëlklip Beach. Heading east towards Stanford and Gansbaai are long, open beaches or secluded coves with patches of sand and rock pools.

The essential whale lexicon

A couple of days along the cliffs of Hermanus is enough to persuade anyone to help save the whale. Here are some useful words to help you convince people of your dedication to the cause.

Breaching Probably the most spectacular sight, this is when whales lift their entire body out of the water in an effortless arc, creating a huge splash as they fall back into the sea. Not an isolated event, a whale will often leap several times so keep your binoculars trained. The experts have yet to agree on why the whale does this and, so far, the whales aren't giving much away.

Blowing This is the sight we are all familiar with – the spout of water vapour accompanied by an echoing sound as air is expelled from their lungs through the blowhole. The seasoned whale watcher will be able to identify the species from the shape of the spout. The vapour is created by condensation when the warm breath comes in contact with the cooler outside air.

Grunting Just a loud grunting noise, which carries a long way over water. It can be a moving sound when heard on a calm, moonlit night. No translations yet available.

Lobtailing The action of a whale slapping the surface with its tails, producing a loud clap. This can be seen repeatedly and over a long time period. It is generally interpreted as some form of warning or social communication.

Sailing Whales lift their tail clear of the water for long periods. There are several theories behind this action: to use the wind to 'sail' through the water, to feed on the sea-floor, or as a means of temperature control. The diehard watchers reckon the whales are just showing off.

Spyhopping When the whale lifts its head and part of its body vertically above the water. This gives the whale a 360 degree view of the seas.

Hermanus Wine Route
Hemel-en-Aarde Valley

Hidden away in the **Hemel-en-Aarde Valley** behind Hermanus is a small collection of vineyards producing some surprisingly good wines, mostly Burgundy varieties based around Pinot Noir and Chardonnay grapes. These smaller and lesser-known wineries are very pleasant to visit since they are rarely crowded and the owners are enthusiastic about their venture. There are three vineyards which are open to the public and have tastings in their cellars. **Hamilton Russell Vineyards** is one of the more picturesque estates. The cellar and tasting room are set beside a small trout lake. (**T** 028-3123595. Closed Sun). **Whalehaven Wines** is the newest vineyard in the valley, and all their wines are quite young. The cellars and the production rooms are open to visitors; a Pinot Noir is their flagship wine (**T** 028-3161633, www.whalehavenwines.co.za Closed Sun).

Betty's Bay
100 km east of Cape Town, 40 km west of Hermanus

Heading west towards Strand is this small holiday village, known for its penguin colony and botanical garden. The village itself is an untidy collection of holiday homes, but the location is beautiful. At Stoney Point there is a reserve to protect a small breeding colony of African penguins, one of the only places other than Boulders Beach in Cape Town where they breed on the mainland. Behind the village are the well-known **Harold Porter Botanic Gardens**, worth a visit for its indigenous flora and colourful birds (**T** 028-2729311, www.mbi.ac.za, daily, 0800-1630, R7).

Stanford
20 km east of Hermanus

This peaceful Victorian village, with its limewashed buildings and slow pace, has become a popular centre amongst artists and craftsfolk. It's a good place to wander around for an hour or so, taking in the well-restored Victorian thatched cottages and beautiful setting right on the Klein River. Nearby is the **Birkenhead Micro-Brewery**, just out of town off the R326 to Caledon (**T** 028-3410183, birkenhd@hermanus.co.za, 1000-1600). There are brewery tours and a pub serving meals and the five beers brewed on-site .

Gansbaai
40 km south of Hermanus

On the eastern end of Walker Bay is Gansbaai, famed for its great white sharks. The village is a prosperous fishing harbour with a modern deep water wharf and several fish canning factories. It has, however, managed to retain the character of a small community and busy fishing harbour, albeit with strong ties to the tourist industry.

There are some good vantage points for whale watching near Gansbaai, most of which are crossed by a 7 km Coastal Walk, including the cliffs at **De Kelders** caves. But the main reason for coming here is **Dyer and Geyser Islands**, important breeding spots for African penguins and Cape fur seals. The narrow canal between the island attracts a number of great white sharks, hence its name: **Shark Alley**. A boat trip here is hugely entertaining – even if you don't see any sharks, you'll see literally hundreds of seals. Cage diving to see the sharks is hugely popular here for those with a diving certificate. However, conservationists argue that these trips can be harmful to the sharks as they interfere with their natural eating patterns and can encourage them to equate humans with food (contrary to popular belief, we do not feature on their standard menu). If you are considering a cage dive, check with the tourist office which is currently the best company running trips – one preferably partaking in conservation and research into the species. There are two seasons for viewing – low season, October through to mid-January and high season. During low season, operators reckon the probability of sightings is about five days out of ten.

Grootbos Nature Reserve
12 km from Stanford

This private nature reserve and luxury camp is a highlight, covering over 1000 ha of fynbos-clad hills. The reserve, which has won several conservation and eco-tourism awards, lies inland from Gansbaai, with stunning views of Walker Bay and the surrounding countryside. It is a beautiful area, and a great chance to spend some time in relative wilderness. Activities available include horse riding and mountain biking trails through the hills, three-hour walks with nature guides, boat trips to Deyer Island and trips to the De Kelders caves. Accommodation is in luxurious individual cottages. **T**028-3840381, www.grootbos.com

Cape Agulhas
36 km south of Bredasdorp

Driving south from the town of Bredasdorp on the R319 you reach Cape Agulhas, the southernmost point of Africa, but it is rather disappointing and lacks the grandeur one might hope for. A soon-to-be completed tarred road may inject some much-needed investment to the area, but for now there's little reason for coming here other than to say you've been.

The Winelands

This was the first region after Cape Town to be settled, making the towns of Stellenbosch, Paarl and Franschhoek some of the oldest in South Africa. Today their streets are lined with beautiful Cape Dutch and Georgian houses, although the real architectural gems are the manor houses on the wine estates. During the 18th and 19th centuries, the farmers built grand homesteads with cool wine cellars. Most of these can be visited during a trip to a vineyard – a few have even been converted into luxury hotels. Hiring a car is the best way of seeing the area; on a long day you could visit all the wineland towns and still catch sunset at Cape Point.

Stellenbosch is 46 km from Cape Town and is served by the Metro railway (1 hr). The N2 takes you along the northern fringes of the Cape Flats. The R310 left turning is the quickest route to the town. The R44 is an alternative route to the heart of the area.

Stellenbosch

Stellenbosch, the centre of the Winelands, is the oldest and most attractive town in the region, and one of South Africa's finest. The town itself is a pleasing mix of architectural styles – Cape Dutch, Georgian, Regency and Victorian houses line broad streets dappled with shade from centuries-old oak trees, and roadside furrows still carry stream water to the gardens. It is the most interesting of the area's towns, and with its handful of museums and lively nightlife, thanks to the university, makes for a good base for visiting the wine estates. The town offers two approaches to sightseeing: walking around the town centre viewing public buildings, oak-lined streets and stately homes; or going on a wine tour, visiting any number of the roughly 100 wineries and private cellars. Spend a couple of days in Stellenbosch and you'll get to do both.

▸▸ *See Sleeping p121, Eating and drinking p150 and Map 8 p256*

Sights

Dorp Street
runs east-west in the southern part of town

Dorp Street is one of the finest in Stellenbosch. It has all the classic features – an avenue of oak trees, running water in open furrows and carefully restored white-walled buildings. A walk from the **Libertas Parva** building to the Theological College takes you through the oldest parts of town and past some of the best preserved buildings. **Libertas Parva**, until recently the Rembrandt van Rijn Art Gallery, is a beautifully restored classic H-shaped manor house built in 1783. Next door, on the corner of Dorp Street and Strand, is the **Stellenryck Wine Museum** (*Mon-Fri 0900-1245, 1400-1700, Sat 1000-1300, 1400-1700*); the small collection of wine-making tools hardly merits a visit.

Instead, continue east along Dorp Street, where you'll pass the famous **Oom Samie se Winkel** (Uncle Sammy's Shop), at number 84. This general store has been trading since 1791, and became famous between 1904 and 1944 when it was owned and run by Samuel Johannes Volsteedt. He stocked virtually everything one could need, and was known throughout the region. Today the shop still sells a wide range of goods and it has retained its pre-war character with items hanging from all corners and old cabinets full of bits and pieces. It has all the makings of a tourist trap, but unlike many others it is genuine.

Look out for the collection of **town houses** just past the junction with Helderberg Street. Hauptfleisch House, at number 153, Bakker House, at number 155, Loubser House, at number

! Stellenbosch was the first European settlement in the interior of Southern Africa when in November 1679 Simon van der Stel left Cape Town to explore the hinterland.

157, and Saxenhof, at number 159, are regarded as the best-preserved street façades in old Stellenbosch.

Branching off from Dorp is **Drostdy Street**, dominated by a tall tower. Also in this street is the town church, the **Moederkerk**; its current steeple was designed by Carl Otto Hagen and built in 1862. Inside it is worth admiring the pulpit and the unusually thick stained-glass windows.

Botanical Gardens
Off Neethling St. *Mon-Fri 0900-1630, Sat 0900-1100.*

The Botanical Gardens are part of the University of Stellenbosch and have a fine collection of ferns, orchids and bonsai trees. One of the more unusual plants to look out for is the *Welwitschis* from the Namib Desert.

Village Museum
Ryneveld St, **T** 021-8872902, www.museums.org.za/stellmus
Mon-Sat 0930-1700, Sun 1400-1700. R15.

The Village Museum is the most interesting sight in Stellenbosch. The complex currently spreads over two blocks in the oldest part of town. There are four houses, each representing a different period of the town's history. The oldest of these is Schreuderhuis (1709), one of the earliest houses to be built in Stellenbosch. Blettermanhuis (1789) is a perfect example of what has come to be regarded as a typical H-shaped Cape Dutch home. The furnishings are those of a wealthy household between 1750-80. The third building is Grosvenor House (1803), in Drostdy Street, an excellent example of the two-storeyed town houses that once dominated the streets of Cape Town. The fourth and final house is the fussy OM Bergh House (1870). All four are set in neat kitchen gardens representing the popular plants of each period. Guides dressed in period clothes are at hand in the houses to answer any questions.

The Braak

Voc-Kruithuis, **T** 021-8864153. *Sep-May Mon-Fri 0930-1630. free.*
Toy and Miniature Museum, **T** 021-8867888. *Mon-Sat 0930-1700,
Sun 1400-1700. R5.*

The Braak, at the western end of Church Street, is where much of
the town's activity takes place. This is the original village green,
and one-time military parade ground. On the western edge by
Market Street is the VOC-Kruithuis, or Powder House, built in 1777
as a weapons store. Today it is a small military museum. Two
churches overlook the Braak: Rhenish Church was built in 1832 as a
training school for coloureds and slaves, and St
Mary's-on-the-Braak is an Anglican church, completed in 1852. A
short distance north, on the corner of Alexander Street, is the
Burgerhuis, a classic H-shaped Cape Dutch homestead built by
Antonie Fick in 1797. A little to the west, on Market St just behind
the Tourist Office, is the Toy and Miniature Museum, a small but
fairly diverting collection of antique toys including a small-scale
working reproduction of the Blue Train. Most interesting is the
small workshop where you can observe the painstaking work of an
onsite expert craftsman producing tiny replicas of clothes and
household items.

Stellenbosch Wine Route

*This was the first wine route to open in South Africa, in April 1971.
It was the idea of three local farmers: Neil Joubert, Frans Malan and
Spatz Sperling. It has been hugely successful, attracting tens of
thousands of visitors every year, and today the membership comprises
around a hundred private cellars. It is possible to taste and buy wines
at all of them, and the cellars can arrange for purchases to be
delivered internationally. Many of the estates have developed
excellent restaurants as well as providing popular picnic lunches
– at weekends it is advisable to book ahead.*

▶ Four Passes route

One of the most popular recommended day drives from Cape Town is known as the Four Passes route. This takes you through the heart of the Winelands, and as the title suggests over four mountain passes. The first stop on the drive is Stellenbosch. From here you take the R310 towards Franschhoek. Driving up out of Stellenbosch you cross the first pass, **Helshoogte Pass**. After 17 km you reach a T-junction with the R45: a left turn would take you to Paarl, 12 km, but the route continues to the right. This is a very pleasant drive up into the Franschhoek Valley, following a railway line and for a part the Berg River. After passing through Franschhoek, take a left in front of the Huguenot Monument and climb out of the valley via the **Franschhoek Pass**. This pass was built along the tracks formed by migrating herds of game centuries earlier, and was originally known as the Olifantspad (elephant's path).

One of the more surprising aspects of the drive is the change in vegetation once you cross the lip of the pass, 520 m above Franschhoek. As the road winds down towards Theewaterskloof Dam you pass through a dry valley full of scrub vegetation and fynbos – gone are the fertile fruit farms and vineyards. Take a right across the dam on the R321 towards Grabouw and Elgin.

The route continues across the Theewaterskloof Dam and then climbs **Viljoens Pass**, the third of four. To the right lies the Hottentots Holland Nature Reserve, a popular area for hiking. The country around here is an important apple growing region.

The fourth and arguably the most spectacular pass is **Sir Lowry's Pass**, which crosses the imposing Hottentots Holland Mountains and provides sweeping views over to False Bay with Table Mountain looming in the background.

Delaire

On the right at the head of Helshoogte Pass, on the R310 towards Franschhoek, **T** 021-8851756, www.delairewinery.co.za *Sales and tastings Mon-Fri 0900-1700, Sat 1000-1700, Sun 1000-1600. Map 8, E3, p256*

This small estate has some of the best views in the valley, and has managed to produce some very high-standard wines. Their flagship Merlot is very popular, while the Chardonnay remains a favourite export label.

Delheim

T 021-8884600, www.delheim.com *Sales and tastings: Mon-Fri 0900-1700, Sat 0900-1530, Sun 1030-1530 (Oct-Apr only). Cellar tours: Mon-Fri 1030 and 1430, Sat 1030. Restaurant open for lunch Mon-Sat 1200-1500, Sun 1200-1500 (Oct-Apr only). Map 8, D3, p256*

Delheim is one of the more commercially orientated estates and may be a little too impersonal for some visitors. However the *Vintner's Platter Garden Restaurant* has a beautiful setting with views towards Cape Town and Table Mountain. Tastings are conducted in a cool downstairs cellar.

Hartenberg

Off Bottelary Rd 10 km north of Stellenbosch, **T** 021-8652541, www.hartenbergestate.com *Sales/tastings: Mon-Fri 0900-1700, Sat 0900-1500. Lunches: Mon-Sat, 1200-1400, closed Sun. Map 8, D2, p256*

Hartenberg is a privately owned old estate, founded in 1692. During the summer, lunches are served in the peaceful gardens; come winter the tasting room doubles up as a restaurant with warming log fires. A variety of red and white wines are produced, but their reds seem the most successful – recent award-winners include their 2000 Shiraz and the 2001 Merlot.

Neethlingshof

4 km west of Stellenbosch, off the M12 (look out for the flag poles), **T** 021-8838988, www.neethilingshof.co.za *Sales and tastings: Mon-Fri 0900-1700, Sat and Sun 1000-1600. Cellar and vineyard tours: by appointment. Lord Neethling and Palm Terrace restaurants open 0900-2100. Map 8, E2, p256*

The long pine-lined avenue and cluster of Cape Dutch buildings make this a pleasant estate to visit, and there are two fine restaurants on site, too. The first vines were planted here in 1692 by a German, Barend Lubbe, and the manor house was built in 1814 in traditional Cape Dutch H-style. Today this has been converted into the *Lord Neethling* restaurant. Neethlingshof has won a clutch of awards – the Lord Neethling Pinotage '98 has won trophies.

Saxenburg

14 km from Stellenbosch, off the M12, close to Kuils River, **T** 021-9036113, www.saxenburg.co.za *Sales and tastings: Mon-Fri 0900-1700, Sat 0900-1600, Sun 1000-1600 (Sep-May only). Guinea Fowl (T 021-9065232) restaurant open daily for lunch and dinner. Map 8, E1, p256*

Saxenberg has a long history, starting in 1693 when Simon van der Stel granted land to a freeburgher, Jochem Sax, although it is only in the last fifteen years that it has been developed into a showpiece on the Wine Route. It produces a small number of cases each year; its Private Collection red wines are very good.

Spier

On the R44, **T** 021-8091100, www.spier.co.za *Sales and tastings: daily 0900-1700. Meals are available throughout the day and evening at 4 on-site restaurants (book several days ahead); picnics and a deli are also available.*

This is the Winelands' most commercial wine estate but offers a vast array of activities and wine tastings – of both Spier's own wines and other Stellenbosch estates'. Spier wines are well regarded, and their Private Collection Chenin Blanc '01 is especially good. As well as wine tasting, there is a cheetah outreach programme (although the creatures seem rather lacklustre) and a birds of prey area, plus horse riding, fishing, golf and a spa. There are four restaurants on site – book ahead. An annual music and arts festival is held at the open-air amphitheatre during the summer months.

Simonsig

T 021-8884900, www.simonsig.co.za *Sales and tastings: Mon-Fri 0830-1700, Sat 0830-1600. Wine cellar tours: Mon-Fri 1000 and 1500, Sat 1000.*

This large estate has been in the Malan family for ten generations, and in recent years has produced some exceptionally fine wines. There is an attractive outdoor tasting area with beautiful views out over the mountains. One wine worth looking out for is the Kaapse Vonkel, a sparkling white considered the best of its kind in South Africa. Their Chardonnay is consistently high quality, and is good value too.

★ Vergelegen Estate

On Lourensford Rd off the R44, **T** 021-8471344, www.vergelegen.co.za *0930-1600. R10, fee includes wine tasting and a cellar tour.* Map 8, G3, p256

Vergelegen Estate is one of the Cape's finest estates, and you should allow several hours for a visit. The highlight is a visit to the magnificent manor house and its octagonal garden. The house is full of period furniture and paintings, similar to the collection at Groot Constantia. Between October and April you can have an alfresco lunch overlooking a collection of rose bushes. The modern cellars are buried on Rondekop Hill, overlooking the estate – there are good views from here of the mountains and False Bay.

Franschhoek

This is the most pleasant of the Wineland villages, with a compact centre of Victorian white washed houses backed by rolling vineyards and the rugged slopes of the Franschhoek Mountains. It does, however, have an artificial feel to it as most of the attractions here have been created to serve the tourist industry. The outlying wine estates all have their individual appeal, but the village itself is made up of restaurants and touristy craft shops. Nevertheless, Franschhoek is famed for its cuisine, so a visit here should guarantee an excellent meal.

▸▸ *See Sleeping, p123, Eating and drinking, p154 and Map 8, p256*

Franschhoek is 71 km from Cape Town (via N1). There is no public transport from Cape Town to Franschhoek. Franschhoek is 26 km from Paarl.

 Sights

Huguenot Memorial Museum and Monument Collection
Lambrecht St. *Mon-Fri 0900-1700, Sat 0900-1300, 1400-1700, Sun 1400-1700. R5.*

This museum is housed in two buildings either side of Lambrecht Street. The main building, to the left of the Huguenot Monument, is modelled on a house designed by the French architect, Louis Michel Thibault, built in 1791 at Kloof Street, Cape Town. The displays inside trace the history of the Huguenots in South Africa and their way of life. There are some fine collections of furniture, silverware and family Bibles, but little to hold one's attention for very long. One of the roles of the museum today is to maintain an up-to-date register of families and their children, so that future generations will be able to trace their ancestors.

Next door to the museum is the unattractive **Huguenot Monument**, a highly symbolic memorial built to mark 250 years since the first Huguenots settled in the Cape. It is set in a peaceful rose garden with the craggy Franschhoek Mountains as a backdrop. The three arches represent the Trinity, and the golden sun and cross on top are the Sun of Righteousness and the Cross of Christian Faith. In front of the arches is a statue of a woman with a Bible in her right hand and a broken chain in her left, symbolizing freedom from religious oppression. If you look closely at the globe you can see several objects carved into the southern tip of Africa: a Bible, harp, spinning wheel and a sheaf of corn and the vine. These represent different aspects of the Huguenots' life, respectively their faith, their art and culture, their industry and their agriculture. The final piece of the memorial, the curved colonnade, represents tranquillity and spiritual peace after the problems faced in France.

Franschhoek Wine Route

*All the vineyards lie along the Franschhoek valley, making it one of the most compact wine routes in the region. What makes this such a rewarding route is that several estates have opened their own excellent restaurants and several also offer luxury overnight accommodation. Note that there are now twenty-six wine estates on the route, with more being added every year. All the valley's wine can be tasted at the **Franschhoek Vineyards Co-operative**, located on the right just before you enter the village when approaching from Stellenbosch (**T** 021-8762086, Mon-Fri 0930-1700, Sat 1000-1600, Sun 1100-1500).*

Boschendal

T 021-8704211, www.boschedalwines.co.za   *Sales and tastings: Mon-Sat 0830-1630; Nov-Apr also Sun 0930-1230. Vineyard tours: 1030 and 1130, by appointment.*   Map 8, D4, p256

Boschendal estate has been growing wine for 300 years and is today one of the most popular estates in the region, not least for its excellent food and pleasant wine-tasting area underneath a giant oak. The estate started life as two farms in 1687, and was bought in 1715 by Abraham de Villiers. Today the main manor house (1812) is open as a museum to the public. Most of the wine produced on the estate is white; their sparkling wines are highly regarded. Interestingly, a third of the estate is now owned by a black empowerment consortium.

La Motte

La Motte, **T** 021-8763119, www.la-motte.co.za   *Sales and tastings: Mon-Fri 0900-1630, Sat 1000-1500. Cellar tours: by appointment.*
Map 8, D5, p256

The original manor house and cellars were built in 1752 and the grand old cellars, worth a visit alone, are now used as a classical concert venue in the evenings. Wine tasting takes place in a smart 'tasting centre' overlooking the cellars. As a relatively small producer, only 15,000 cases per annum, the estate has managed to create some excellent wines. The La Motte Millennium Claret blend remains their most popular wine.

L'Ormarins

T 021-8741026, www.lormarins.co.za   *Sales/tastings: Mon-Fri 0900-1630, Sat 0900-1500. Cellar tours: by appointment.*   Map 8, D4, p256

L'Ormarins vineyard has a beautiful setting on the slopes of the Drakensteinberge. The present homestead was built in 1811 – from its grand marble halls and staircases you look out across an ornamental pond and neat mature gardens. The other notable attraction is the original wine cellar; this has been carefully restored and now houses a set of giant wine vats. On offer is the classic range of wines, plus the Italian varietal range, Terra del Capo.

Paarl

*While Paarl is home to two of South Africa's better-known wine estates, **KWV** and **Nederburg**, the town itself is not as interesting as Stellenbosch or as fashionable as Franschhoek. All of the attractions and restaurants are strung out along Main Street at the base of **Paarl Mountain**. When the first European, Abraham Gabbema, saw the mountain in October 1657 it had just rained; the granite domes sparkled in the sunlight and he named the mountains paarl (pearl) and diamandt (diamond). The town grew in a random fashion along an important wagon route to Cape Town. Several old buildings survive, but they are spread out rather than concentrated in a few blocks like Stellenbosch. Paarl is, however, a delightful place to watch an international cricket match in a peaceful rural setting. A good braai and some fine local wines make for a perfect day out.*

▸▸ *See Sleeping p125, Eating and drinking p156 and Map 8 p256*

There are regular metro trains between Cape Town and Paarl, but only use these during rush hour (0600-0800, 1600-1800).

 Sights

Paarl Museum and around
Main Street, **T** 021-8762651. *Mon-Fri 0900-1700, Sat 0900-1300. R5.* Afrikaans Language Museum, **T** 021-8723441. *Mon-Fri 0900-1700. R5.*

The 1-km walk along Main Street will take you past most of the finest buildings in Paarl. Here you'll find one of the oldest buildings, the **Paarl Museum**, at 303 Main Street. This houses a reasonably diverting collection of Cape Dutch furniture. There is also a small section outlining Paarl during apartheid, although the fact that Nelson Mandela spent his final years in prison near Paarl is barely mentioned. Only a few hundred metres away, in Gideon Malherbe House, on Pastorie Street, the **Afrikaans Language Museum** gives a detailed chronicle of the development of the Afrikaans language and the people involved.

Near Lady Grey Street is **Zeederberg Square**, a 19th-century square with a fine mix of restored buildings and lively restaurants. Further south on Main Street is the **Strooidakkerk**, a thatched roof church, consecrated in 1805 and still in use. It stands in a spacious churchyard full of flowers and cypress trees. It was designed by George Küchler – note the gables, a sounding-board to amplify sermons and the fine pulpit. You may have to ask for a key from the church office.

Arboretum

Open during daylight hours. From the Publicity Office, go down Market St, cross the river and it is on the right.

On the east bank of the Berg river is the 31-ha arboretum. There are over 700 different species in a total of 4,000 trees. The grounds have been divided into six sections, each containing species from different continents.

● *The best views of the surrounding countryside are from Bretagne Rock; on a clear day you can see False Bay, Table Mountain and all the vineyards.*

! Nelson Mandela spent his final years in prison near Paarl. His first steps of freedom were from Victor Verster Prison, 9 km south of Paarl.

Taal Monument
Daily 0800-1700. R5.

Set high on the slopes of Paarl Mountain amongst granite boulders
and indigenous trees stands the controversial Taal Monument –
three concrete columns linked by a low curved wall. This is the
Afrikaans language monument, inaugurated in October 1975 and
designed by Jan van Wijk. Each column represents different
influences in the language. The relative heights of each column
and the negative connotations associated with them have been
the subject of criticism in recent years. There is a coffee shop with
excellent views across the Berg River Valley.

Butterfly World
Klapmuts, **T** 021-8755628. *0900-1700. R25, children R12.50.*

Those with kids in tow may wish to visit Butterfly World, the largest
such park in South Africa, with butterflies flying freely in colourful
landscaped gardens. Craft shop and tea garden.

Paarl Wine Route

*The route was set up in 1984 by local producers to help promote their
wines and attract tourists into the area. The programme has been a
great success and some of the estates have opened their own
restaurants, but don't expect discounts on the wine with your meal.
Today there are 29 members offering tastings and sales; only the
largest estates conduct regular cellar tours.*

Boland Kelder
On the R45 towards Wellington, **T** 021-8626190,
www.bolandwines.co.za *Sales and tastings: Mon-Fri 0800-1700, Sat
0830-1300. Cellar tours: by appointment.* *Map 8, A4, p256*

Boland Kelder estate has an excellent wine cellar, and offers one of the most interesting cellar tours. One of their best wines is the 2002 Chardonnay, which has won awards.

Fairview Wine Estate
South on the R45, right on to the R101, then first right.
T 021-8632450, www.fairview.co.za *Wine and cheese sales and tastings: Mon-Fri 0830-1700, Sat 0830-1300. R12 for cheese tastings. Map 8, C3, p256*

This is a popular estate with a rather unusual attraction in the form of a goat tower, a spiral structure home to two pairs of goats. In addition to a variety of very good wines – look out for the popular Goats do Roam and their 2000 Chardonnay – visitors can taste goat and Jersey milk cheeses. The goats are milked each afternoon from 1530.

Laborie
Just outside Paarl by the railway station. **T** 021-8073390, www.kwv-international.com *Sales and tastings: daily, 0900-1700, closed Sun from May-Oct. Cellar tours: by appointment. Map 8, C4, p256*

The Laborie vineyard, part of KWV (see below), is a beautifully restored original Cape Dutch homestead – in many ways the archetypal wine estate, and developed with tourism firmly in mind. It's an attractive spot, with a tasting area overlooking rolling lawns and vineyards, and a highly-rated restaurant.

KWV
T 021-8073900, www.kwv-international.com *Sales and tastings: Mon-Sat 0900-1630. Cellar tours: Mon-Sat 1000, 1015 (in German), 1030, 1415. Map 8, C4, p256*

A short distance from the Laborie estate is the famous KWV Cellar Complex which contains the five largest vats in the world. The Ko-operatieve Wijnbouwers Vereniging van Zuid-Afrika (Co-operative Wine Growers' Association) was established in Paarl in 1918 and is responsible for exporting many of South Africa's best-known wines. They are also well known for their brandy.

Nederburg
Off the R303 towards Wellington, **T** 021-8623104, www.nederburg.co.za *Sales and tastings: Mon-Fri 0830-1700, Sat 1000-1600, Sun 1100-1600. Map 8, B4, p256*

Nederburg is one of the largest and best-known estates in South Africa with an annual production in excess of 650,000 cases. Every April the annual Nederburg Auction attracts buyers from all over the world and it is considered one of the top-five wine auctions in the world. The homestead was built in 1800, but throughout the 19th century the wines weren't considered to be anything special. Today their wines win countless annual awards – the 2003 Sauvignon Blanc and the 2001 'Petit Verdot' are recent examples.

Villieria
On the R101, off the R304 to Stellenbosch, **T** 021-8652002, www.villiera.co.za *Sales and tastings: Mon-Fri 0830-1700, Sat 0830-1300. Cellar tours: by appointment. Map 8, D1, p256*

Villieria is highly regarded and produces some of the best wines in the Cape. There are plenty of classic wines to choose from, including the Cru Monro, the Merlot 2001 and their Sauvignon Blanc. They no longer conduct cellar tours, but allow self-guided tours.

The city centre and surrounds offer an excellent selection of accommodation, from exclusive vineyard estates and fashionable boutique hotels, to cosy seaside guesthouses and edgy backpacker lodges. Accommodation tends to be good value for money, and despite the strengthening Rand it is possible to find some bargains, especially out of season. Prices vary considerably, but there's something to suit every budget. A luxurious suite on a historical estate can cost as much as R4,000 a night; a comfortable town hotel should be no more than R1,000, while smaller guesthouses and B&Bs are usually between R300 and R800. Backpacker hostels can be as cheap as R60.

The City Bowl is the most popular area with visitors, but there is also a good range along the coasts and in the suburbs. The Winelands are becoming famous for their luxurious estate-based guesthouses, and the Whale Coast has a good range of B&Bs. Bear in mind that the Cape is extremely popular, especially over Christmas, so be sure to book several months in advance.

Sleeping codes

Price

AL	R1,500 and over		**E**	R90-180
A	R750-1,500		**F**	less than R90
B	R480-750		Price of a double room	
C	R300-480		excluding service charges	
D	R180-300		and meals	

The city centre

Hotels

AL Mount Nelson, 76 Orange St, Gardens, **T** 021-4231000, www.mountnelsonhotel.orient-express.com *Map 2, D5, p248*
Cape Town's most famous hotel, grand old colonial building with 131 luxurious rooms, 28 suites and eight garden cottage suites. Rooms have all the mod cons but can be too old-fashioned for some. Set in landscaped parkland with heated swimming pool, tennis courts, squash court and beauty centre. Celebrated *Cape Colony* restaurant serves Cape specialities and contemporary fare to live jazz. Well worth visiting, if only for the daily cream teas on the veranda.

A Cape Cadogan, 5 Upper Union St, **T** 021-4808080, www.capecadogan.com *Map 2, E4, p248*   New addition to the city's boutique hotels, ultra-elegant mansion with 12 rooms, all large with grass mat flooring, private terraces, subtle lighting and decor, big four-poster beds, interesting touches like drift-wood chandeliers, fabulous bathrooms, some with enormous stone walk-in showers for two. Shady courtyard with small pool, all-white dining room with pleasant breezes.

A Kensington Place, 38 Kensington Gardens, Higgovale, **T** 021- 4244744, www.kensingtonplace.co.za *Map 2, G2, p248* Stylish boutique hotel in a quiet, leafy area. Small and well-run with excellent and friendly service. Eight beautiful and good-sized rooms, each individually styled with a mix of ethnic and ultra-chic furnishings, big bathrooms, lots of light from the large windows, great views over the city, bar, pool and tropical gardens, breakfast served on a leafy veranda, excellent restaurant. Recommended.

A Metropole , 38 Long St, **T** 021-4247274, www.metropolehotel.co.za *Map 2, A8, p249* This overhauled hotel brings some Met-style fashion to the city centre. Forty-five double rooms with understated decor, huge beds, attractive dark-wood furniture and abstract prints on the walls. Beautiful stone bathrooms with bath and shower. The *M Bar & Lounge* has become a trendy after-work drinks place, and with its red ostrich-leather chairs and subdued lighting feels more like Manhattan than South Africa. Elegant restaurant on first floor serves a mix of Italian and modern South African cuisine. Excellent and friendly service. Recommended.

A Villa Belmonte, 33 Belmont Av, Oranjezicht, **T** 021-4621576, www.villabelmontehotel.co.za *Map 2, H5, p248* Luxury Italian-style villa with 14 rooms, old fashioned with heavy fabrics and plush furnishings, TV, mini bar, large shady veranda with spectacular views of Table Mountain and the city bowl. Good breakfast buffet served in smart restaurant, lunch and dinner also available. Spacious swimming pool and attractive garden.

B Ikhaya Guest Lodge, Dunkley Sq, Gardens, **T** 021-4618880, www.ikhayalodge.co.za *Map 2, D7, p249* A smart, African-themed guesthouse a short distance from the city centre with 11 double rooms, five apartments for self-catering guests. Full of character thanks to the natural woods, African fabrics and recycled decorations (the bedside lamps are made from old ginger beer bottles).

B park inn, 10 Greenmarket Sq, **T** 021-4232050,
www.parkinn.com *Map 2, A8, p249*   Brand new, large, city centre
hotel set in the historical Shell building right on bustling
Greenmarket Sq. The rooms have pleasant, neutral decor and
functional, attractive bathrooms (shower only). Small pool deck
with sauna and gym with view of Table Mountain. Good restaurant
– *The Famous Butcher's Grill* – on ground floor with tables
overlooking the market, plus pleasant, if dark, cigar bar. Excellent
service, perfect central location and secure parking. A practical
and comfortable choice.

B Tudor Hotel, Greenmarket Sq, Centre, **T** 021-4241335,
www.tudorhotel.co.za *Map 2, A7, p249*   Recently refurbished hotel
in historic building on Greenmarket Sq. Choice of 26 modern but
fairly bland doubles and family rooms with TV. All have en suite
trendy bathrooms with shower, some have air-conditioning.
Breakfast served in stylish downstairs café, off-street parking
available for R45 per day. Great location.

B Underberg Guest House, 6 Tamboerskloof Rd, **T** 021-
4262262, www.underbergguesthouse.co.za *Map 2, C3, p248*
Attractive old corner house with decorative iron balconies, 11
spacious rooms, some are rather dated but others have been
tastefully refurbished, en suite bathrooms, TV and mini bar, shared
veranda with mountain views, full English breakfast, laundry
service, convenient for city centre, friendly and helpful owners.

C Ambleside Guest House, 11 Forest Rd, Oranjezicht,
T 021-4652503, F 4620690 *Map 2, H4, p48*   Quiet house set on
a leafy road with bright, comfortable rooms, some with views of
Table Mountain, pleasant solid wood furniture and neutral decor.
Family rooms available. Breakfast served at a table in your room.
Friendly service.

C **Leeuwenvoet House**, 93 New Church St, Tamboerskloof, **T** 021-4241133, www.leeuwenvoet.co.za *Map 2, D4, p248* Ten double rooms, all en suite, comfortable homely decor, wrought-iron beds, some have air-conditioning, TV, telephone, excellent breakfasts, swimming pool, off-street secure parking, close to shops and restaurants but retains a peaceful atmosphere.

C **Table Mountain Lodge**, 10a Tamboerskloof Rd, **T** 021-4230042, www.tablemountainlodge.co.za *Map 2, C3, p248* Characterful house with seven beautifully decorated rooms, stripped wooden floors, white linen, large spotless bathrooms, breezy and very comfortable, small garden with splash pool, breakfast room, tiny bar called 'Jock's Trap', owned by the very friendly Diana and Janne Dagh. Highly recommended.

C-D **Parker Cottage**, 3 Carstens St, Tamboerskloof, **T** 021-4246445, www.parkercottage.co.za *Map 2, C4, p248* Award-winning B&B, stylish and atmospheric set in a restored Victorian bungalow, eight bedrooms, en suite roomy bathrooms with claw-foot baths, polished wood floors, lots of antiques, flamboyant colours with a Victorian touch, good breakfasts, friendly service, gay-friendly. Recommended.

Hostels

F **Ashanti Lodge**, 11 Hof St, Gardens, **T** 021-4238721, www.ashanti.co.za *Map 2, E6, p248* Cape Town's best-known and most popular hostel, not least for its party atmosphere. Medium-sized dorms and small doubles in huge old house with polished wooden floors, large windows and communal balconies. Some rooms surround a courtyard and small pool. Lively bar serving good snacks, with pool table and TV M-Net. Free airport and station pickup, excellent booking centre, internet and video room. Firmly on the busy overland truck route, can be very noisy (and bathrooms get rather messy), but perfect for meeting people. Also has a guesthouse (**D**) nearby with smart en suite double rooms and spotless kitchen.

F   The Backpack, 74 New Church St, Centre, **T** 021-4234530, **F** 4230065, www.backpackers.co.za *Map 2, C5, p248*   One of the original Cape Town hostels, this is one of the most comfortable and best-run in town. Set across several houses with spotless dorms, doubles and en suite doubles and singles. Polished wood floors, upmarket decor, tiled courtyard and linked gardens with pool, lovely bar with TV, meals and snacks served throughout the day, one of the best backpacker travel centres around. Recommended.

F   Cat & Moose Youth Hostel, 305 Long St, Centre, **T** 021-423 7638, catandmoose@hotmail.com *Map 2, C6, p248*   Bright set-up, central location in an atmospheric old town house. Dorms and doubles are nicely furnished but a bit dark, those at front can be noisy, some have balconies overlooking Long Street. Lovely courtyard with sun deck and braai, good bar, small travel centre, TV/video lounge. Laid-back, friendly atmosphere.

F   Long St Backpackers, 209 Long St, Centre, **T** 021-4230615, longstbp@mweb.co.za *Map 2, B7, p249*   Lively and sociable hostel spread around leafy courtyard, small clean dorms and doubles, some with own bathrooms and balconies overlooking Long St, fully equipped kitchen, TV/video lounge, pool room, internet access, travel centre, free pickup. Good security with 24-hour police camera opposite. Lively atmosphere, occasional parties organized and weekly communal braais, but can be noisy.

F   Oak Lodge, 21 Breda St, Gardens, **T** 021-4656182, www.oaklodge.co.za *Map 2, F7, p249*   Beautiful Victorian house which started out as a commune and was developed into a hostel several years ago. The hippie vibe continues throughout. Large, attractive dorms, comfortable doubles (some in bungalow next door), great showers, relaxed bar, chill-out room, two video rooms and a homely kitchen. Decor is an interesting mix of African masks, ethnic fabrics and medieval wall murals.

F Overseas Visitors Club, 230 Long St, Centre, **T** 021-4246800, www.ovc.co.za *Map 2, C6, p248* Expect a warm welcome at this unlikely looking place above the *Maharaja* Indian restaurant. Clean and comfortable, if a little small and lacking the atmosphere found in larger hostels. Great balcony with braai overlooking Long St and views of Table Mountain, bar, excellent travel centre upstairs specializing in youth travel. One of the friendliest on Long St.

F Zebra Crossing Backpackers, 82 New Church St, Centre, **T/F** 021-4221265, zebracross@intekom.co.za *Map 2, C4, p248* Quiet, friendly backpackers straddling two Victorian bungalows, with spotless dorms plus small double rooms, good views of Table Mountain, internet access and travel centre. There's a shady courtyard café and bar serving great breakfasts, snacks and meals. Helpful management.

Victoria and Alfred Waterfront

Hotels

AL Cape Grace, **T** 021-4107100, **F** 4197622, www.capegrace.com *Map 3, D11, p251* This has become one of the most luxurious hotels in Cape Town. It's a large development, just a short walk from the main Waterfront shops and restaurants. The very comfortable rooms have all mod cons, traditional decor and balconies with views of the Waterfront. Service and food is excellent in the two bars and the celebrated *one.Waterfront* restaurant. There's also a swimming pool and deck with bar.

AL Table Bay Hotel, Quay 6, Waterfront, **T** 021-7807878, **F** 7807061. *Map 3, B11, p251* Enormous luxury offering from the Sun International Group, 329 top-notch rooms, what they lack in character they makeup for in facilities and comfort. Large pool and sundeck, health club and spa, bar and good restaurant. Expensive by Cape Town standards, efficient service but feels a tad ostentatious (note the sculpture outside the main entrance with plaques commemorating the stays of celebrities and politicians).

A Victoria & Alfred, Pierhead, **T** 021-4196677, www.vahotel.co.za *Map 3, C10/11, p251* Stylishly converted warehouse with 68 rooms, spacious with cool and comfortable furnishings, king-size beds, air-conditioning, TV with DVD player, mini-bar, dramatic mountain views, large marble and stone bathrooms with separate WC. Excellent restaurant serving seafood and steaks, fashionable, airy bar attached. Friendly and efficient service. Recommended.

B-D Breakwater Lodge, Portswood Rd, **T** 021-4061911, www.breakwaterlodge.co.za *Map 3, C9, p251* This hotel, owned by the university (a number of MBA students live here in term time), fills what was once the notorious Breakwater Prison (1859). The 268 rooms are fairly small with functional corporate-style decor. Restaurant, conference centre, good setting close to the Waterfront and the nightlife in Green Point.

Atlantic Seaboard

Hotels

AL-A The Bay Hotel, Victoria Rd, Camps Bay, **T** 021-4384444, www.thebay.co.za *Map 5, E3, p253* Set just across the road from the beach, member of the Small Luxury Hotels of the World, with

70 modern deluxe air-conditioned rooms, all with views across the bay, pleasant contemporary feel, large pool with deck and beach-facing restaurant with a good reputation. Excellent service, a well-known place for the rich and famous.

A The Clarendon, 67 Kloof Rd, Sea Point, **T** 021-4393224, www.clarendon.co.za *Map 4, F3, p252* Luxurious Italian-style guesthouse with 10 spacious rooms spread across main house and garden suites, plus extra house further up the street. Rooms are large and grandly furnished with posh bathrooms, some with great views of Lion's Head. Attractive garden with large pool shaded by banana trees, breakfast served on terrace, beautiful lounge, off-street parking. Elegant and peaceful place to stay, family-friendly, recommended. Also has new guesthouse by Camps Bay at no. 158 Kloof St.

A Le Vendome, 20 London Rd, Sea Point, **T** 021-4301200, www.le-vendome.co.za *Map 4, B5, p252* A large, well-designed luxury hotel with a French theme. Traditional and very comfortable rooms and suites with air-conditioning, TV and internet facilities. Attractive courtyard with pool, 1 restaurant overlooks the pool and serves snacks and lunch, the other is for fine dining. Secure parking.

A Peninsula, 313 Beach Rd, Sea Point, **T** 021-4307777, www.peninsula.co.za *Map 4, E2, p252* 'Timeshare Hotel' with 110 suites, all with balconies, sea views and self-catering kitchenettes. Large, modern tower right by the sea with friendly and efficient service, bar, restaurant serving light lunches and buffets in the evenings, two swimming pools, gym, games room for children. The penthouse suites have jacuzzis and braai balconies overlooking the sea. Great location in Sea Point, a short walk from all the shops and restaurants.

A-B Winchester Mansions, 221 Beach Rd, Sea Point, **T** 021-4342351, www.winchester.co.za *Map 4, A6, p252* A well-run family hotel with a range of rooms from old-style chintz to newly designed and chic. All rooms have TV, en suite bathroom with separate shower, some with views of the Altantic. Pleasant pool deck and new Ginkgo Spa. All rooms overlook a large, tranquil courtyard were meals are served beneath the palms. Also has *Harvey's* restaurant, serving fusion cuisine and Sunday jazz brunches.

A-C De Waterkant Lodge & Cottages, 20 Loader St, Green Point, **T** 021-4222721, www.villageandlife.com *Map 3, F9, p251* This is more of a mini-empire than a guesthouse: *Village and Life* own over 50 historical Bo-Kaap style houses and apartments in the trendy Waterkant area, each stylishly and individually decorated, sleeping from one to six. Also has *Waterkant House*, a guesthouse with nine comfortable, chic rooms with all mod cons, a splash pool, beautiful lounge and terrace. Other main property is *House of the Traveller*, a 'luxury' backpackers with double rooms and shared bathroom and kitchen. Other properties available across Cape Town. A fantastic range, offering convenient accommodation in stylish and historical buildings. Highly recommended.

B Cape Victoria, 13 Torbay Rd, Green Point, **T** 021-4397721, www.capevictoria.co.za *Map 3, D6, p250* A mix of exclusive hotel service and the privacy of a guesthouse. Ten tastefully furnished rooms with antiques, en suite bathrooms, TV, mini bar and views of the sea or Table Mountain, swimming pool, booking essential. Run by the affable Lilly. Recommended.

B The Glen Guest House, 3 Glen Rd, Sea Point, **T** 021-4390086, www.glenhotel.co.za *Map 4, C5, p252* Thoroughly overhauled boutique hotel in an Italian-style villa with views of Signal Hill. Classy decor and super-trendy bathrooms, some with two-people showers. Tropical garden with palm trees, pool and shaded seating areas, Moroccan-themed steam room with splash pool. Secure parking. Note that this a gay hotel, as a staff-member snarled on our most recent visit.

B Monkey Valley, Mountain Rd, Noordhoek, **T** 021-7891391, www.monkeyvalleyresort.com *Map 1, F2, p246* Luxurious resort with self-catering thatched log cottages set in woodland overlooking Noordhoek Bay. Each sleeps from four to eight people, with two or free bedrooms, kitchen, lounge and bathroom spread across two floors, plus secluded veranda with superb views.

B-C Blackheath Lodge, 6 Blackheath Rd, Sea Point, **T** 021-4392541, www.blackheathlodge.co.za *Map 3, D2, p250* Seven smart double rooms in a converted Victorian mansion. Off-street parking, TV, mini bar, palm-fringed patio, swimming pool, but no children under 14. Recommended for couples.

B-C t'Huijs Haerlem, 25 Main Drive, Sea Point, **T** 021-4346434, www.huijshaerlem.co.za *Map 3, E3, p250* 2 beautifully converted neighbouring houses with four rooms in each, connected by well-tended gardens. All rooms are en suite, with solid antique furniture, brass beds, some four-poster beds, big bathrooms, fabulous sea views. Solar heated salt-water swimming pool. Both houses have breakfast rooms and lounge – one decorated with Dutch furniture, the other in South African style. Very friendly Dutch owners. Highly recommended.

C Brenwin Guest House, 1 Thornhill Rd, Green Point, **T** 021-4340220, www.brenwin.co.za *Map 3, D7, p251* Recently renovated guesthouse with 14 large, well-appointed rooms with en suite bathrooms, wooden floors, simple decor, shady patio overlooking tidy tropical garden with swimming pool, within easy walking distance of the Waterfront. Owners Uwe and Pam are very helpful.

C Villa Rosa, 277 High Level Rd, Sea Point, **T** 021-4342768, www.villa-rosa.com *Map 4, 6D, p252* Rose-coloured Victorian villa with eight bright and comfortable rooms, traditional, appealing furnishings, original fireplaces, new stone-tiled bathrooms, all rooms en suite with TV, some with fridges, one family room and one 'flatlet'. Brilliant breakfasts served with home-made breads and jams. Off-street parking, pleasant veranda with sea views. This is a supremely friendly, welcoming and relaxed place to stay. Highly recommended.

C Whale Cottage Guesthouse, 57 Camps Bay Drive, Camps Bay, **T** 021-4383840, www.whalecottage.com *Map 5, H9, p253* Small tasteful place with marine decor, four sunny double rooms with en suite bathrooms, breakfast deck overlooking the beach, good views of the Twelve Apostles, satellite TV and internet access, five minute's walk to the shops and beach. Also has another property in nearby Bakoven and Hermanus on the Whale Coast.

C-D Bay Atlantic, 3 Berkley Rd, Camps Bay, **T** 021-4384341, www.thebayatlantic.com *Map 5, D4, p253* Family-run guesthouse with some of the best views in Cape Town. Six en suite rooms, TV, light and airy with terracotta tiles and white linen, some with private balcony, stunning views of Camps Bay and the Twelve Apostles. Also has two self-catering apartments next door. Quiet garden with good-sized pool, breakfast served on balcony overlooking the bay, relaxed atmosphere. Run by the friendly and welcoming Smith family. Great value, highly recommended.

C-D Dune Lodge , cnr Northshore Drive & Victoria Ave, Hout Bay, **T** 021-7905847, www.dunelodge.co.za *Map 1, E2, p246* Great location on dunes overlooking Hout Bay. Six double rooms with en suite bathrooms, TV, bright and breezy with new bathrooms, great views, pleasant glassed-in veranda, popular holiday guesthouse. Also has family unit sleeping four.

D Bellevue Manor House, 5 Bellevue Rd, Sea Point,
T 021-4340375, www.bellevuemanor.co.za *Map 4, C6, p252*
Range of double and self-catering rooms in a beautiful Victorian
town house on a quiet side street. Main house has wrought-iron
balconies and fine palm trees, all rooms have en suite bathrooms,
homely decor, TV, non-smoking, laundry service.

D Kinneret Guest House, 11 Arthur's Rd, **T** 021-4399237, Sea
Point, kinneret@iafrica.com *Map 4, D5, p252* Lemon-yellow
Victorian house close to the sea with 10 rooms, bright but with
heavy curtains and dark bedspreads, en suite bathrooms, fridge,
TV and telephone. Family-run, comfortable, short walk from sea
and shops.

Hostels

C-F Aardvark Backpackers , 319 Main Rd, Sea Point,
T 021-4344172, www.lions-head-lodge.co.za/aardvark.htm
Map 4, B6, p252 Upmarket backpackers centrally located close to
restaurants and shops, also known as *Lions Head Lodge*. The lodge
side has 37 comfortable en suite hotel rooms with TV, available at
a backpackers rate. The dorms are located in former self-catering
flats so each six- to 12-bed dorm has its own kitchen and
bathroom. Restaurant, lodge bar, beer garden, backpackers bar, TV
lounge, library, pool, informative travel centre and internet café,
can book all day tours and specializes in overland tours to Nairobi.
Friendly set-up. Recommended.

F St John's Waterfront Lodge, 6 Braemar Rd, Green Point,
T 021-4399028, stjohnslodge@mweb.co.za *Map 3, E8, p251*
Closest hostel to the Waterfront. One of the first hostels in Cape
Town, quiet spot compared to other backpackers, dorms and
doubles, fully equipped kitchens, restaurant and sea views.

F Stans Halt Youth Hostel, The Glen, Camps Bay , **T** 021-4389037, stanh@new.co.za *Map 1, C2, p246* A great, cheap alternative amongst the super-wealthy. Fabulous location in small nature reserve high above Camps Bay. Five basic dorms with six beds in each, lounge, kitchen, pleasant veranda beneath trees, building is surrounded by woods, bicycle hire, very popular in season. Rumours of a move soon, so call in advance to check. Great place – easy to forget you're in a big city.

F Sunflower Stop, 179 Main Rd, Sea Point, **T** 021-4346535, **F** 4346501, www.sunflowerstop.co.za *Map 4, E4, p252* Dorms with more room than most, doubles, clean place with a huge kitchen. Swimming pool, bar, satellite TV, tours and travel advice. Good location close to restaurants and bars. Free airport and city pick up.

Southern Suburbs

Hotels

AL The Cellars-Hohenhort, 93 Brommersulei Rd, Constantia, **T** 021-7942137, www.cellars-hohenhort.com *Map 1, D3, p246* Part of the Relais & Chateau group. One of the most luxurious hotels in Cape Town, set in two converted manor houses on a wine estate, with 13 spacious suites and 33 individually decorated double rooms, plus the newly built Madiba Presidential Suite. All are thoughtfully decorated, with huge beds, antiques and spacious bathrooms. Two excellent restaurants (see p143). Conference facilities, two swimming pools, tennis court, golf course, impeccable service.

AL-A Constantia Uitsig, Spaanschemat, River Rd, Constantia, **T** 021-7946500, www.constantiauitsig.co.za *Map 1, D3, p246* Set on the well-known wine estate, with 16 luxurious and spacious cottages set in neat gardens with views across vineyards to the mountain. Plush furnishings, private verandas, variety of activities on offer including horse riding and vineyard walks. Two restaurants, food is excellent, book ahead.

AL-A Steenberg Country Hotel, 20 km from Cape Town in the Constantia Valley, **T** 021-7132222, www.steenberghotel.com *Map 1, D3, p246* Luxurious country hotel with 30 elegant, traditional rooms furnished with beautiful antiques, in converted farm buildings overlooking manicured gardens and working vineyards. Swimming pool, gym, steam room, horse riding and 18-hole golf course. *Catharina* restaurant has excellent reputation. Relaxed and friendly atmosphere.

A Alphen Hotel, Alphen Dr, **T** 021-7945011, www.alphen.co.za *20-mins' drive from the city centre, located at the head of Constantia Valley*. *Map 1, D3, p246* Thirty-four spacious rooms on elegant 18th-century Cape Dutch estates. Suites and rooms are decorated with fine antiques, beautiful rugs on polished floors and log fires during winter months. Lunches are served in a pub or in the gardens during the summer, and in the evening there is a popular restaurant in the Manor House which attracts many non-residents. Swimming pool and free use of a nearby sports centre.

A The Vineyard Hotel, Protea Rd, Newlands, **T** 021-6574500, www.vineyard.co.za *Map 1, C4, p246* Air-conditioned rooms in a large 18th-century house; the decor is early Cape Dutch with yellow-wood furniture. Coffee shop and pâtisserie, elegant restaurant, swimming pool and old gardens. One of the best-value upmarket hotels in Cape Town.

B Harfield Cottage, 26 1st Avenue, Claremont, **T** 021-6837376, www.harfield.co.za *Map 1, C4, p246* Award-winning, elegant B&B with individually designed, quirky rooms. All are spacious, en suite, with TV, mini bar and views of Table Mountain. Lounge/bar, sundeck and swimming pool, bicycle hire, secure off-street parking. Relaxing ambience during the winter months when log fires keep guests warm. Recommended.

C Devonshire House, 6 Lovers Walk, Rondebosch, **T/F** 021-6861519, *Map 1, C4, p246* Restored house with five double rooms, all with en suite bathroom, TV, friendly service, garden with pool. The old wooden floors greatly add to the homely atmosphere.

Hostels

F The Green Elephant, 57 Milton Rd, Observatory, **T** 021-4486359, www.hostels.co.za *Map 7, A2, p255* A full-on backpacker joint set in an old Observatory mansion, plenty going on in the area away from the city centre, dorms plus five double rooms, some en suite, with four-poster beds in a separate house, also a long-stay house, garden with pool and jacuzzi, small bar, pool table, TV room, laundry facilities. Happy to organize trips to the regional sights, free collection. Helpful and knowledgeable staff, owned by the enthusiastic Robin who is keen to introduce visitors to voluntary projects available for visits in Cape Town. Recommended budget option.

F SA's The Alternative Place, 64 St Michaels Rd, Claremont, **T/F** 021-6742396, www.alternativeplace.co.za *Map 1, C4, p246* Clean dorms sleeping four, plus two double rooms, kitchen, garden with pool, bar and braai. A small homely set-up run by Susan and Alun who have excellent southern and east African travel experience. A bit far from the town centre, but worth checking out. Free airport pickup service.

False Bay

Hotels

A Quayside Hotel, Quayside Centre, Wharf St, Simon's Town, **T** 021-7863838, www.quayside.co.za *Map 1, I3, p247* A smart, newish development in a great location overlooking the harbour and right in the centre of town. The marine-style double rooms are comfortable, bright and sunny with good views but are rather over-priced. Book well in advance for visits during local holidays.

B Southern Right , 12-14 Glen Rd, Glencairn, **T** 021-7820314, info@southernright.info *Map 1, H3, p247* New, delightful hotel in turn of the century building set back from the sea. Eight double and twin en suite rooms (another 10 are being added) with high ceilings, dark polished wood floors, subtle decor, four-poster beds, some with baths only, others with shower and bath. Stylish bar and restaurant serving pub meals, seafood and grills. Fashionable place but family friendly. Recommended.

B-C British Hotel Apartments, 90 St George's St, Simon's Town, **T** 021-7862214, www.british-hotel.co.za *Map 1, I3, p247* Despite the unpromising name, this is one of the best places to stay in False Bay. Converted characterful Victorian hotel with four elegant self-catering apartments. Each apartment is enormous, stretching over two open-plan floors, with three bedrooms, all en suite with delightful Victorian bathrooms. Polished wood floors throughout, attractive mix of maritime antiques, art deco and stylish modern furnishings, open-plan kitchen and lounge, separate TV room, great views of the bay from magnificent balconies, breakfasts available on request. Highly recommended.

B-C Tudor House by the Sea, 43 Simon's Town Rd,
T 021-7826238, www.tudorhouse.co.za *Map 1, I3, p247* Six luxury
self-catering apartments with between one and three bedrooms,
friendly and very reasonably priced. Apartments have all mod cons,
serviced daily, secure parking, secluded gardens, ideal for a longer
break for those wishing to explore the area, very popular in season,
advance reservations necessary.

C Boulders Beach Guest House, 4 Boulders Place,
T 021-7861758, www.bouldersbeach.co.za *Map 1, I3, p247*
This friendly, well-run guesthouse is a firm favourite with us.
Twelve double rooms with en suite bathrooms, most arranged
around a paved yard (without sea view), simple refreshing design,
just metres from the beach. Also has two self-catering apartments.
At night you're likely to see penguins exploring the grounds after
everyone has gone home.

C-D Sonstraal Guest House , 4 Axminster Rd, Muizenburg,
T 021-7881430, www.sonstraalguesthouse.com *Map 1, F4, p246*
Pleasant guesthouse a short walk from the beach and seafront.
Seven en suite rooms in the main house, plus self-catering
cottages sleeping four to six and studios sleeping two. Simple
decor, spotless rooms and bathrooms, sunny breakfast room,
plant-filled courtyard, pool. Run by a friendly Dutch couple.
Good discounts offered out of season.

Hostels

E-F Top Sail House, 176 St George's St, Simon's Town,
T 021-7865537, slodon@homechoice.co.za *Map 1, I3, p247*
Quiet backpacker's hostel set in an old convent school building,
peaceful place with ordinary dorms, doubles, balcony overlooking
St George's St, bike hire, friendly.

F Simon's Town Backpackers, 66 St George's Mall, Simon's Town, **T** 021-7861964, www.capepax.co.za *Map 1, I3, p247*
Forty-bed backpacker joint spread across cramped dorms and fairly pleasant doubles, brightly painted walls and bush-camp-style furniture, small kitchen, honesty bar, braai on balcony overlooking the main street and harbour, bikes for hire.

The Whale Coast

Hermanus

A The Marine, Marine Drive, **T** 028-3131000, www.collectionmcgrath.com Part of the Relais & Chateaux group. Forty-two luxurious rooms, some with stunning ocean views, all with exceptionally fine furnishings – silk curtains, plush carpets, pale suede armchairs and marble bathrooms. Also has a spa, heated swimming pool, shop, internet access and two restaurants; the seafood restaurant was voted the best in South Africa in 2004. Recommended for a treat.

B Auberge Burgundy, 16 Harbour Rd, **T** 028-3131201, www.auberge.co.za. Provençal-style villa in the heart of Hermanus, with 17 rooms, a mix of doubles and suites, all set around a smart inner courtyard with a swimming pool, private terraces or balconies, some with fine views across Walker Bay. Also owns the *Burgundy* restaurant, opposite. Good reports from some readers.

B Windsor Hotel, 49 Marine Drive, **T** 028-3123727, www.windsor-hotel.com Large and popular hotel set on cliffs overlooking the ocean. Sixty en suite rooms with TV, some have sea views. Excellent views across Walker Bay from the glassed-in lounge. Slightly plain restaurant. Frequently used by tour groups, small boat hire service.

C Kenjockity, 15 Church St, **T** 028-3121772, kenjock@hermanus.co.za A typical old Hermanus house which started life as a boarding house in the 1920s. Thoughtfully restored with 14 rooms, some with en suite bathroom, country-style furnishings, bright colours, friendly and helpful owners, within walking distance of the sea and shops.

D-F Zoete Inval, 23 Main Rd, **T** 028-3121242, www.zoete inval.co.za Excellent budget choice with three double rooms, two family rooms and a converted loft with two dorms. Pleasant TV lounge, self-catering kitchen, laundry, secure parking. Will meet the Baz Bus at *Bot River Hotel* for small fee. Friendly and good value.

F Moby's Backpackers, 8 Main Rd, **T** 028-3132361, www.mobys.co.za Backpackers' joint offering a good range of rooms: doubles, dorms sleeping six to eight, family rooms, all are en suite. Pub with satellite TV, large garden with pool, daily braais, internet access, TV lounge, fully equipped kitchen. Friendly and laid-back place, do Baz Bus pickups for small fee. Also organizes cheap shark dives, as well as wine tasting, sandboarding and the usual choice of excursions.

The Winelands

Stellenbosch

L Lanzerac Manor, Jonkershoek Rd, **T** 021-8871132, www.lanzerac.co.za *Map 8, E2/3, p256* Very expensive but fittingly luxurious hotel set around an 18th Cape Dutch manor house. Forty-eight rooms, some around a patio and swimming pool, spacious and plush with all the mod cons. Two restaurants: the formal *Governer's Hall*, which is rather fussy with slow service; and the relaxed and more enjoyable *Taphuis*.

A d'Ouwe Werf, 30 Church St, **T** 021-8874608,
www.ouwewerf.com *Map 8, E2/3, p256* Converted Georgian
house with 31 air-conditioned rooms, all individually decorated
with antique furnishings, some with four-poster beds, all with
attractive tiled bathrooms with free-standing bath. Polished floors,
off-street parking, good-sized pool and vine-shaded terrace where
breakfast and lunch are served. Restaurant *1802* offers traditional
Cape cooking in smart surroundings, and has had good reports.
Recommended as a treat.

A The Village at Spier, Spier Wine Estate on the R44,
T 021-8091100, www.spier.co.za *Map 8, F2, p256* Probably the
Winelands' most commercial wine estate, but a thoroughly
enjoyable place to stay. Accommodation is in a set of condo-style
buildings set around courtyards with private pools. Rooms are
enormous and very comfortable, with neutral, stylish decor, trendy
polished concrete floors, huge beds, lots of windows, TV, mini-bar,
beautiful bathrooms stocked with aromatherapy products. Four
restaurants on site.

A-B Stellenbosch, 162 Dorp St, **T** 021-8873644,
stb-hotel@mweb.co.za *Map 8, E2/3, p256* Central hotel with
27 air-conditioned rooms and two apartments in a National
Monument building. Each room has TV, mini-bar and pleasant
bathrooms, although the decor could do with an update. Friendly
bar popular with locals, bright dining room with tables on terrace
overlooking the street serving game and seafood.

B De Goue Druif, 110 Dorp St, **T** 021-8833555, http://gouedruif
.hypemart.net *Map 8, E2/3, p256* Guesthouse in a National
Monument building. Four well-appointed if old-fashioned rooms
(lots of ruffs and heavy curtains), spacious bathrooms, lush garden
with pool and terrace, plus tiny gym, steambath and sauna. Secure
parking. Friendly service. Ideal location for exploring town on foot.

B Dorpshuis, 22 Dorp St, **T** 021-8839881, **F** 8839884,
www.dorphuis.co.za *Map 8, E2/3, p256* Twenty-two
air-conditioned rooms, some of which are suites, all have TV,
marble-clad bathrooms, heavy fabrics and dark furniture, private
patios, antiques, large breakfasts with plenty of choice, neat
gardens, swimming pool, a very smart Victorian town house.

C Wilfra Court, 16 Hine St, **T/F** 021-8896091, **T** 082-9200085
(mob). *5 km from the centre, off the R44 road to Paarl.* *Map 8, p256*
Two double rooms with shared bathroom, breakfast included, run
by William and Francis. Anyone with an interest in South African
political affairs should stay here. This was the first guesthouse in the
region run by coloured people and William was an MP for more than
30 years. Strongly recommended. A unique experience.

F Stumble Inn, 12 Market St, **T** 021-8874049, stumble@iafri
ca.com *Map 8, E2/3, p256* Popular hostel in two separate old Cape
houses. Spacious double rooms and cramped dorms. Original
house has attractive garden, bar, TV room, kitchen, hammocks;
other house has a small pool. By far the best budget option.

Franschhoek

AL-A Auberge du Quartier Français, corner of Wilhelmina
and Berg St, **T** 021-8762151,www.lequartier.co.za *Map 8, E6,
p256* An elegant country house with 14 large en suite rooms all
with fireplaces and pleasant views over the gardens. Small central
swimming pool and peaceful courtyard. The attached restaurant is
rated as one of the best in the country, but the food can be fussy
and disappointing. Nevertheless, a good hotel for a treat.

B Auberge La Dauphine, PO Box 384, **T** 021-8762606,
www.ladauphine.co.za *Map 8, E6, p256* One of the most peaceful
locations in the valley. Five luxury rooms each with a spacious

lounge in a carefully restored and converted wine cellar. The house is surrounded by beautiful gardens and vineyards. Large swimming pool, guided tours of the farm, plus mountain bike trails and horse riding in the nearby mountains.

B La Cabriere, Middagkrans Rd, **T** 021-8764780, www.lacabriere.co.za *Map 8, E6, p256* Small luxurious and stylish guesthouse set just outside town in formal lavender and herb gardens. Five air-conditioned rooms with Provençal decor, limed wood furniture, grass matting floors and large stone en suite bathrooms. Two rooms are in the main house and the rest in separate building with guest lounge, breakfast room and pool. Understated and stylish spot in a peaceful location.

B-C Résidence Klein Oliphants Hoek, 14 Akademie St, **T** 021-8762566, www.kleinoliphantshoek.com *Map 8, E6, p256* A very fine guesthouse close to the centre. Seven old-fashioned air-conditioned double rooms with en suite bathrooms and TV (M-Net). The vast, high-ceilinged lounge is filled with antiques, big sofas and a fireplace. Good-sized pool. Very smart dining room with a daily changing set menu serving excellent French cuisine (R225 per person for four courses). Friendly service.

C La Fontaine, Main Rd, **T** 021-8762112, www.lafontaine franschhoek.co.za *Map 8, E6, p256* One of the finest guesthouses in Franschhoek. Nine rooms set in a Victorian house near the village centre, elegant decor with antiques and fine wooden floors, large Victorian-style bathrooms. Some rooms set in garden around pool with 'ethnic' decor. Lovely vine-shaded courtyard where breakfast is served. Friendly, excellent value and a beautiful place to stay, run by Kathie and Stella. Highly recommended.

C Le Jardinet, 3 Klein Cabriere St, **T/F** 8762186, regeorge@ mweb.co.za *Map 8, E6, p256* Peaceful, family-run B&B in quiet side street. Two double rooms with en suite bathroom, one with a yellow theme, the other blue. Spotless bathrooms, homey atmosphere, beautiful gardens overlooked by shady veranda where breakfast is served. Guest lounge has a library, fridge, TV and video player. We've had consistently positive reports of this place.

D-F La Bri Holiday Farm, Robertsvlei Rd, **T** 021-8763133. *Map 8, p256* Choice of self-catering cottages which can sleep up to six, or dormitory, peaceful rural location, braais, child-friendly, swim in the farm dam, must have your own transport to get here.

Paarl

AL Grande Roche, Plantasie St, **T** 021-8632727, www.granderoche.com *Map 8, B4, p256* An 18th-century manor has established itself as one of the top hotels in South Africa with luxury air-conditioned suites and no-smoking rooms. A collection of restored farm buildings stand in peaceful gardens, surrounded by vineyards, two floodlit tennis courts, two swimming pools, gym. *Bosman's* restaurant is regarded as one of the best in South Africa.

L-A Zomerlust, 193 Main St, **T** 021-8722117, **F** 8728312, www.zomerlust.co.za *Map 8, B4, p256* Fourteen rooms in a restored historical country house in the centre of town. All rooms are en suite, with TV, fireplaces and decked out in antiques. Some rooms are in converted stables. Courtyard, terrace, library, swimming pool, cellar pub and popular attached restaurant – *Kontreihuis*. Check for winter discounts.

A Roggeland Country House, Roggeland Rd, Dal Josafat, **T** 021-8682501, www.roggeland.co.za *Map 8, B4, p256* A fine Cape Dutch farmhouse (declared a National Monument) with 10 spacious luxury rooms, large en suite bathrooms, Cape style furnishings, mature gardens, swimming pool. Highlight of a stay here is the excellent cuisine: lodging prices include dinner, bed and breakfast.

B Lemoenkloof Guest House, 396a Main St, **T** 021-8723782, lemkloof@adept.co.za *Map 8, B4, p256* Luxurious converted country house on northern edge of town. Twenty air-conditioned rooms grouped in several buildings set around gardens and a palm-shaded pool. Each room has TV, mini bar, floral fabrics, fresh flowers in vases, black-and-white tiled bathrooms, separate entrance. Large breakfasts, evening meals on request, friendly.

B Palmiet Valley, **T** 021-8627741, www.palmiet.co.za *Map 8, B4, p256* A restored historic Cape Dutch homestead located on an estate to the east of the town centre. Ten spacious double rooms with en suite bathrooms, TV, CD player, each decorated with antiques, private balconies or terraces, neat garden, swimming pool.

C Nantes-Vue, 56 Mill St, **T** 021-8727311, www.nantes-paarl.co.za *Map 8, B4, p256* Elegant B&B set in a Victorian house in the centre of town. Four double rooms and one-bedroom cottage in garden, all with high ceilings, natural fabrics, iron bedheads, grass matting floors, beautiful bathrooms with enormous showers and free-standing baths, breakfast room has country farm feel to it, lovely lounge with big leather sofas. Hosts, Patricia and James, offer a warm welcome to guests. Good value. Recommended.

C-E Amberg Guest Farm, Klein Drakenstein, **T** 021-8620982, amberg@mweb.co.za *Map 8, B4, p256* Good budget option on farm with spectacular setting. Two self-catering cottages, plus one apartment sleeping four to six. Gardens, large pool, braai facilities, friendly Swiss owners (German and French spoken).

Sleeping

Cape Town likes to eat out, and with good reason. The city is blessed with spectacular outdoor eating locations, a multitude of superb restaurants and a standard of cooking usually only found at break-the-bank prices in Europe. Summer is the most popular time for eating out, and the Waterfront, perhaps the city's most popular eating area, gets very busy. Booking ahead is often a good idea and essential on Saturday nights.

Just about every restaurant offers fresh, good-value seafood – locally caught snoek, kingclip and crayfish are reliable options. Meat lovers are also well served: South Africans are serious carnivores, with steaks and exotic game such as ostrich or springbok featuring on most menus. Vegetarians, however, may have a harder time. Although Cape Town is more sympathetic to meat-free dining than most of the country, choices remain limited. There is a handful of vegetarian restaurants, though, and these are generally very good.

Eating codes

Cape Town offers a full range of international restaurants, from French bistros and sushi bars to Mozambique seafood. Its local cuisine is Cape Malay cooking, an interesting blend of curries softened with coconut milk and fruit. Although there are surprisingly few Cape Malay restaurants, some of the more popular dishes such as bobotie, a sweet-spicy dish of minced beef, is served in many mainstream restaurants. A local term to listen out for is braai, quite simply cooking food on a barbecue, usually accompanied by copious quantities of alcohol. Braais are incredibly popular and in summer are a major form of entertainment for Capetonians. The staple diet for most South Africans is stiff maize porridge, known as pap, and served with stew. It is not a dish that tourists are likely to encounter unless invited into an African home, although a handful of 'traditional' African restaurants in town serve pap with game.

The city centre

Restaurants

ᵞᵞᵞ **Aubergine**, 39 Barnet St, Gardens, **T** 021-4654909, www.aubergine.co.za *Mon-Sat 1800-2200*. *Map 2, D8, p249* One of the best in town. Sophisticated and award-winning menu, offering modern slants on classical European dishes, plus an excellent wine list and good service. Tables are in a stylish, shaded courtyard or the lounge/bar. Recommended.

¶¶¶ Blue Danube, 102 New Church St, Tamboerskloof, **T** 021-44233624, www.bluedanube.co.za *Tues-Fri 1200-1430, Mon-Sun 1830-2300.* *Closed Sun and Mon lunch.* *Map 2, C4, p248* Chef Thomas Sinn combines traditional Austrian dishes with an international fusion menu, served in a fine old building with spacious rooms and mountain views.

¶¶¶ Cape Colony, Mount Nelson Hotel, 76 Orange St, Centre, **T** 021-4831000. *1800-2200.* *Map 2, D5, p248* One of Cape Town's finest restaurants in the impressive setting of the *Mount Nelson*. Dishes are a mix of traditional British (think sensible roasts) and Cape classics, such as Bo-Kaap chicken and prawn curry. Impeccable service, live jazz most evenings. Don't miss the high teas on the outside terrace, held every afternoon.

¶¶ The Africa Café, Heritage Sq, 108 Short Market St, Centre, **T** 021-4220221, www.africacafe.co.za *1830-2300.* *Map 3, H10, p251* Upmarket and tourist-friendly restaurant offering an excellent introduction to the continent's cuisines The menu is a set 'feast' and includes 10 dishes that rove around the continent, from Malawian Mbatata balls to Cape Malay mango chicken curry. The price includes the chance to order more of the dishes you like, as well as coffee and dessert. Good value and excellent service, although very touristy.

¶¶ Five Flies, 14 Keerom St, Centre, **T** 021-4244442, info@fiveflies.co.za *1100-midnight.* *Map 2, B7, p249* This is a long-standing local favourite in a historical setting, and its recent restyling has made it even more popular. Appealing string of dining rooms, high standards of traditional fare, cigar lounge. Preferred haunt of lawyers and judges.

★ Al fresco restaurants

Best
- Table Mountain cafeteria, p135
- Quay Four, V & A Waterfront, p137
- Silver Tree, Southern Suburbs, p143
- Black Marlin, Miller's Point, p145
- The Brass Bell, Kalk Bay, p146

🍴 **Kotobuki**, 3 Mill St, Gardens, **T** 021-4623675. *1230-1400, 1830-2200, weekends dinner only*. *Map 2, E6, p248* Japanese, no-frills top-class menu, expensive for Cape Town, but a favourite amongst the Japanese community.

🍴 **Mama Africa**, 178 Long St, **T** 021-4248634. *Mon-Sat 1900-late*. *Map 2, B7, p249* Popular restaurant and bar serving 'traditional' African dishes often with great live music. Popular with tourists, tasty food if overpriced and notoriously slow service. Centrepiece is a bright green carved Mamba-shaped bar. Somewhat tacky but a fun place nonetheless.

🍴 **Rozenhof**, 18 Kloof St, Gardens, **T** 021-4241968. *Mon-Sat 1200-1500, 1800-2200, closed for lunch on Sat*. *Map 2, C5, p248* Smart restaurant set in an attractive 18th-century town house, decorated with local artwork and chandeliers, food to match the surrounds, sensible light dishes full of flavour, look out for seasonal dishes such as asparagus and salads, good choice for vegetarians.

🍴 **Saigon**, corner Camp and Kloof sts, Gardens, **T** 021-4247670, zenasia@iafrica.com *1200-1430, 1800-2230*. *Map 2, E4, p248* Superb Vietnamese cuisine, very popular place overlooking busy Kloof St, brilliant crystal spring rolls, barbecued duck and caramelized pork with black pepper. Book ahead. Recommended.

Eating and drinking

¶¶ **Sukhothai**, 12 Mill St, Centre, **T** 021-4655846. *Mon-Sat 1800-2230*. *Map 2, C6, p248* Good Thai cuisine, set menus for the confused, advisable to book at the weekend, authentically hot and spicy.

¶¶ **Yindee's**, 22 Camp St, Tamboerskloof, **T** 021-4221012, yindees@mweb.co.za *Mon-Sat 1230-1430, 1830-2200*. *Map 2, E4, p248* An excellent Thai restaurant serving authentic spicy curries and soups. Served in a sprawling Victorian house with traditional low tables. Service can be very slow, but the place is always popular, so book ahead.

¶ **Arnold's**, 60 Kloof St, Gardens, **T** 021-4244344, www.arnolds. co.za *1200-late*. *Map 2, D4, p248* Good value lunch spot on busy Kloof Street, good salads, pasta and more substantial meals like ostrich steak. Fast, friendly service.

¶ **Biesmiellah**, 2 Upper Wale St, Centre, **T** 021-4230850. *Mon-Sat 1200-1500, 1800-2200*. *Map 2, A6, p248* One of the better known and well established Malay restaurants, serving a delicious selection of Cape Malay dishes. This is the place to come for sweet lamb and chicken curries and sticky malva pudding. A treat for any fan of spicy food. No alcohol. Recommended.

¶ **The Crypt**, 1 Wale St, below St George's Cathedral, **T** 021-4249426. *Mon-Sat 0830-2300*. *Map 2, B8, p249* Despite its suspect location, this restaurant has lovely sunny tables set out on Wale St and serves the usual sandwiches and salads plus interesting daily pasta specials. Perfect for people-watching in the summer, or huddling in the vaulted interior in winter. Live music in the evenings.

¶ **Marco's African Place**, 15 Rose St, Centre, **T** 021-4235412, www.marcosafricanplace.co.za *1200-late*. *Map 3, H10, p251*

★ Best

Cafés

- Mr Pickwicks, Long Street, p133
- Crush, St Georges Mall, p134
- New York Bagels, Sea Point, p141
- Obz Café, Observatory, p144
- Olympia Café, Kalk Bay, p148

African menu, live music, huge, smoky place with a friendly atmosphere, excellent starters but main courses are disappointing.

❦ **Miller's Thumb** , 10b Kloof Nek Rd, Gardens, **T** 021-4243838. *Mon-Sat 1230-1400, 1830-2230, no lunch Mon or Sat.* *Map 2, D4, p248* Beloved by locals, this place serves delicious and good value seafood, plus steaks and other dishes. Friendly, laid-back place, lots of regulars.

❦ **Mr Pickwicks**, 158 Long St, Centre. *Mon-Sat 0800-0200, Sun 0800-1900. Map 2, B6, p248* Trendy spot serving the best milkshakes in town, excellent French loaf sandwiches, healthy salads, large pasta portions, licensed, gets very busy with an after-work crowd, open late. Also sells tickets to Cape Town's major club nights and gigs.

❦ **Ocean Basket**, 75 Kloof St, Gardens, **T** 021-4220322. *1100-2200. Map 2, D5, p248* A successful, good value franchise serving seafood and salads, pleasant setting with a large courtyard at the back. Fantastically cheap compared to most Cape Town seafood. No bookings, expect to queue outside on the street.

❦ **Primi Piatti**, Greenmarket Sq, Centre, **T** 021-4247466. *Mon-Fri 0800-1800, Sat 0800-1500. Map 2, A8, p249* Lively spot overlooking the square from the huge open windows. Superb pizzas, vast bowls of imaginative pasta and salads, all freshly made, huge portions at reasonable prices, popular with a young fashionable crowd. Also has outlets at Camps Bay and the Waterfront. Recommended.

♀ **Royale**, 273 Long St, **T** 021-4224536. *1100-late. Map 2, B6, p248* Ultra-trendy eatery specializing in gourmet burgers – try the 'Miss Piggy' with bacon and guacamole, served with sweet potato fries. Also has daily pasta specials. Friendly service, popular place, expect to queue.

♀ **yum**, 2 Deer Park Dr, Vredehoek, **T** 021-4617607. *1000-2300. Map 2, H8, p249* Stylish deli and restaurant serving excellent sandwiches, salads and original pasta dishes, such as roast lamb tortellini or goat's cheese and roasted pepper lasagne. Good service, relaxed young crowd, delicious pickles and chutneys on sale. Recommended.

Cafés

♀ **Café Zanne**, 138 Long St, Centre, **T** 021-2429250. *Mon-Fri 0630-1600. Map 2, A7, p249* Standard range or toasted sandwiches, filled baked potatoes and a salad buffet. Mediterranean theme.

♀ **Charly's Bakery**, 20 Roeland St, Centre, **T** 021-4615181, *Mon-Fri 0700-1600 Map 2, C8, p249* Tiny café serving brilliant cakes, pastries and pies – don't miss the spinach and feta pie or the gooey dark chocolate brownies.

♀ **Crush**, 100 St Georges Mall, **T** 021-4225533. *0900-1700. Map 2, A8, p249* Lunch spot spilling onto St Georges Mall serving delicious and healthy wraps, salads and freshly squeezed juices. Live street music provides the entertainment.

Best

★ **Seafood restaurants**

- Baia, V & A Waterfront, p135
- Blues, Camps Bay, p138
- The Codfather, Camps Bay, p138
- Fish on the Rocks, Hout Bay, p140
- Bertha's, Simon's Town, p145

🍴 **Portobello**, 111 Long St, Centre, **T** 021 4261418. *Mon-Fri 0800-1700, Sat 0900-1500*. *Map 2, A7, p249* Vegetarian café and deli serving good quiches, sandwiches, pies and a salad buffet, plus great smoothies and fruit juices.

🍴 **Table Mountain Cafeteria**, Table Mountain, **T** 021-4248181, www.tablemountain.co.za Overpriced and hectic cafeteria, but in one of the best locations imaginable. Self-service sandwiches, cold drinks, ice creams and hot meals. Also sells beers that you can take outside to watch sunset.

Victoria and Alfred Waterfront

Restaurants

🍴🍴🍴 **Baia**, top floor, Victoria Wharf, **T** 021-4210935. *1200-1500, 1900-2300*. *Map 3, B11, p251* Fine seafood restaurant spread over 4 terraces with moody, stylish decor and lighting. Very smart (and expensive) venue, delicious seafood dishes following a Mozambique theme – try the spicy beer baked prawns. Very stylish with views of Table Mountain, slightly erratic service. Book ahead.

🍴🍴🍴 **Emily's**, Clock Tower centre, **T** 021-4211133. *Mon-Sat 1200-1500, 1800-2200*. *Map 3, C10, p251* Very smart restaurant serving excellent French-style cuisine, superb wine list, has won several awards, great views from balcony overlooking the Waterfront, polite service, slightly fussy but remains popular.

⁋⁋ Balducci's, ground floor, Victoria Wharf, **T** 021-4216002, www.balduccis.co.za *0900-2230*. *Map 3, B11, p251* Popular, elegant Italian restaurant with seats overlooking the harbour. Good choice of pasta dishes and mains ranging from ostrich steak and luxury lamb burgers, to confit de canard and blackened kingclip. Also has sushi bar.

⁋⁋ Cantina Tequila, Quay 5, Victoria Wharf, **T** 021-4190207, www.cantinatequila.com *1000-late*. *Map 3, B11, p251* Full range of Mexican dishes, good cocktails, live music Wednesday-Sunday, outside terrace, touristy, indifferent service and erratic food.

⁋⁋ Cape Town Fish Market, ground floor, Victoria Wharf, **T** 021-4135977, 1100-2300. *Map 3, B11, p251* Popular fish restaurant, but the reason to come here is the revolving sushi bar, serving excellent sushi and sashimi. Dishes on offer are limited but very fresh and good value.

⁋⁋ Den Anker, Pierhead, **T** 021-4190249, www.denanker.co.za *0900-2300*. *Map 3, C10, p251* Popular Belgian (Flemish) restaurant and bar, continental feel, high ceiling flying the various duchy flags, newspaper plastered pillars, airy bar, views across Alfred Basin of Table Mountain, civilized atmosphere. Plenty of Belgian dishes to sample plus an amazing selection of imported bottle beers.

⁋⁋ Hildebrand, Pierhead, **T** 021-4253385, www.hildebrand.co.za *1100-2300*. *Map 3, C10, p251* Well-established Italian seafood place right on the harbour's edge. Superb hand-made pasta and good antipasta, plus divine traditional Italian desserts. Good reputation but touristy.

★ **Child-friendly restaurants**

Best

- Dunes, Hout Bay, p140
- Fish on the Rocks, Hout Bay, p140
- Bertha's, Simon's Town, p145
- Penguin Point Café, Boulders Beach, p146
- La Maison de Chamonix, Franschhoek, p155

🍴 **Mortons on the Wharf**, upstairs, Victoria Wharf,
T 021-4183633, www.mortons.co.za *1200-1500, 1800-2300.*
Map 3, B11, p251 A busy New Orleans-style restaurant and bar,
Creole fish dishes or spicy Cajun country food, a playful and fun
evening with live music, Jazz, Mardi Gras and Blues, check out the
Sunday Jazz brunch.

🍴 **Quay Four**, **T** 021-4192008. *1100-late. Map 3, B11, p251*
Pleasant bar-restaurant set on a shady deck overlooking the
harbour. Very popular for seafood lunches served in individual
frying pans, and a good spot for drinks at sundown. Also has a
smarter bistro on the first floor (1800-2230), seafood is the main
focus but also has grills and vegetarian options.

Cafés

🍴 **Mugg & Bean**, Victoria Wharf, **T** 021-4196451. *0830-2330.*
Map 3, B11, p251 Also branches in Cavendish Sq, Claremont, and
the Lifestyles centre on Kloof St. Café serving mouth-watering
muffins, cakes and sandwiches and good coffee. Service can be slow.

🍴 **vida e caffe**, Victoria Wharf, **T** 021-4249440. *0800-2100. Map 3,
B11, p251* Also branch on Kloof St. Espresso bar serving full range
of caffeine-rich beverages, plus pastries, sandwiches and
scrumptious Portuguese custard tarts.

Eating and drinking

137

Atlantic Seaboard

Restaurants

¶¶¶ **Blues**, Victoria Rd, Camps Bay, **T** 021-4382040. *1200-2300. Map 5, E3, p253* Popular and well-known seafood place with superb views, Californian-style menu served to a beautiful crowd. Good, stylish food, the seafood is the best and the oyster platters are famous, but you pay for the restaurant's reputation.

¶¶¶ **The Codfather**, corner Geneva Drive and The Drive, Camps Bay, **T** 4380782. *1200-1700, 1800-2300. Map 5, F3, p253* One of the best seafood restaurants in Cape Town, stylish laid-back place offering a range of superbly fresh seafood. No menu – the waiter takes you to a counter and you pick and choose whatever you like the look of. Also has an excellent sushi bar. Highly recommended.

¶¶¶ **The Restaurant**, 51a Somerset Rd, Green Point, **T** 021-4192921. *Map 3, G10, p251* Superb seafood and meat dishes in a stylish and understated setting. Brilliant desserts and attentive service. Very popular so booking essential.

¶¶ **Buena Vista Social Café**, Main Rd, Green Point, **T** 021-4330611. *1200-0200. Map 3, D8, p251* Cuban-themed bar and restaurant in a great location with balconies overlooking Main Rd. Fashionable, well-heeled crowd tuck into to a mix of Cuban and Tex-Mex-style dishes washed down with mojitos. Live Latin music at weekend, good but pricey.

¶¶ **Camel Rock**, Scarborough, **T** 021-7801122. *1200-1700, 1900-2300. Map 1, I2, p247* A Mediterranean-style seafood restaurant. Sit out on the balcony and enjoy the oysters or excellent calamari, bring your own wines, good stop for lunches.

♯♯ **Mr Chan**, 178a Main Rd, Sea Point, **T** 021-4392239. *1200-1200, 1800-2230. Map 4, C5, p252* Popular local Chinese place serving good quality Peking, Cantonese and Szechuan meals. Good value set meals available.

♯♯ **L'Orient**, 50 Main Rd, Sea Point, **T** 021-4343458. *Mon-Sat, 1800-2330, evenings only. Map 3, D2, p250* Indonesian and Malaysian restaurant, popular and authentic serving a wide range of Asian dishes, quite pricey but with good value set menus. The *Rijsttafel* has 17 individual dishes.

♯♯ **Ocean Blue**, Victoria Rd, Camps Bay, **T** 021-4389838, blufish@mweb.co.za *1200-2200. Map 5, E3, p253* Friendly seafood restaurant on road overlooking the beach. Excellent fresh seafood, especially daily specials, superb grilled prawns and butterfish kebabs. Less pretentious than many of the restaurants in the area.

♯♯ **San Marco**, 92 Main Rd, Sea Point, **T** 021-4392758. *Mon-Sat 1800-2200, Sun 1200-1400, 1800-2200. Map 3, D1, p250* A long-term Sea Point favourite. Extensive Italian menu specializing in seafood. Excellent anitpasto, plenty of vegetarian options, wonderful desserts.

♯♯ **Tuscany Beach**, 41 Victoria Rd, Camps Bay, **T** 021-4381213, www.tuscanybeach.co.za. *1000-late. Map 5, D3, p253* Italian seafood overlooking the beach. Delicious seafood specials – don't miss the kingclip kebabs served on a dangling sword. Also serves wood-fired pizzas, salads, burgers and steaks. Chic place, gets very busy for sundowners.

♯ **Chapman's Peak Hotel**. Hout Bay, **T** 021-7901036, *1100-2200. 0800-late. Map 1, E1, p246* A lively restaurant and bar, fairly old-fashioned but serving good seafood dishes in frying pans, also grills and pub fare. The outside terrace gets packed in summer – be sure to book ahead.

¶ **Chariots**, 107 Main Rd, Green Point, **T** 021-4345427. *1000-2200.*
Map 3, D8, p251 Excellent local Italian restaurant serving
traditional and innovative pasta dishes (try the curried butternut
ravioli), superb risotto, salads and meat dishes. Low-key and
relaxed, good service, tables overlooking Main Rd, popular with
young professionals. Excellent value for money. Recommended.

¶ **Clifton Beach House**, 4th Beach, Clifton, **T** 021-4381955.
0800-2300. Map 5, A1, p253 Breakfast, lunch and dinner
overlooking Clifton's beautiful beach, good seafood plus some
Thai dishes, relaxed during the day but more elegant at night.

¶ **Dunes**, Hout Bay Beach, **T** 021-7901876,
dunes@worldonline.co.za *0900-late. Map 1, E1/2, p246* Sprawling
restaurant overlooking the dunes behind the beach, very popular
with families, large menu, quick service but the food can
disappoint – stick to the tasty fish and chips.

¶ **Fish on the Rocks**, Harbour Rd (beyond Snoekies Market),
Hout Bay, **T** 021-7900001. *1000-2100. Map 1, E1, p246* Simple
and delicious fresh fish and chips, deep-fried calamari and prawns,
overlooking harbour. No frills.

¶ **The Nose**, Cape Quater, Dixon Street, Green Point,
T 021-4252200, www.thenose.co.za *Mon-Sat 1000-2300,*
Sun 1700-2200. Map 3, F9, p251 Wine bar with tables spilling
onto the trendy Waterkant piazza, serving a wide range of wines
accompanied by excellent seafood (the mussels in white wine and
cream are especially good), steaks and burgers. Cosy interior,
dishes can be ordered in large or small portions.

¶ **Red Herring**, Chapman's Bay Trading Centre, Beach Rd,
T 021-7891783. *1000-1500, 1800-2100. Map 1, C1, p247*

Bar upstairs and à la carte restaurant downstairs. Big steaks, plus grilled fish and calamari steak. Sea views make it a great spot for a sundowner.

¶ **Wangthai**, 105 Paramount Pl, Green Point, **T** 021-4396164. *Sun-Fri 1200-1430, 1800-2300, Sat 1800-2300. Map 3, C6, p250* Great Thai restaurant serving mouth-watering stir fries and spicy curries with coconut milk and lemon grass. Reservations advised.

Cafés

¶ **Café Erté**, 265 Main Rd, Sea Point, **T** 021-4346624. *1000-0400. Map 3, D2, p250* Trendy café playing loud trance and techno, good breakfasts and snacks, internet access.

¶ **Dirty Dick's Tavern**, Harbour Rd, Hout Bay, **T** 021-7905609. *1100-late. Map 1, E1, p246* Beer garden and restaurant with open-air terrace overlooking the marina. Steaks, fish and salads.

¶ **Marc's Deli Bar**, Shop 16, The Promenade, Camps Bay, **T** 021-4382322. *0800-2100. Map 5, E3, p253* Smart first-floor deli and café overlooking beach, serving wonderful pastries, muffins and cakes as well as selling a fine selection of breads and cheeses.

¶ **News Café**, corner Main Dr and Ashstead Rd, Green Point, **T** 021-4346196. *0700-2300. Map 3, D7, p251* Popular café and bar chain, serving sandwiches, salads, pub meals, stylish decor, gets busy in the evenings.

¶ **New York Bagels**, 51 Regent Rd, Sea Point, **T** 021-4397523. *0700-2230 (deli closes at 2130). Map 4, F3, p252* Cafeteria-style deli serving a good range of meals, from hearty American breakfasts and smoked salmon bagels through to salads, hotdogs and fish and chips. Attached deli shop next door sells bagels and other Jewish tit-bits to take away.

Rumblin' Tum, Shoreline Centre, Hout Bay, **T** 021-7902047.
0800-1830. Map 1, E1/2, p246 Family coffee shop and restaurant
serving good breakfasts (delicious muesli and yoghurt), but small
portions. Mix of light lunches, outside terrace, sluggish service.

Southern Suburbs

Restaurants

Au Jardin, Vineyard Hotel, Colinton Rd, Newlands,
T 021-6574500, www.vineyard.co.za *Mon-Sat 1900-2200. Map 1,
C4, p246* A very smart hotel restaurant with one of the best French
menus in Cape Town. Six-course meals or a quick plat du jour
served in a stylish setting with views of the mountain. Polite
service, excellent presentation. The best local ingredients turned
into the best European recipes. Recommended. Booking advised.

Buitenverwachting, Klein Constantia Rd, Constantia, **T** 021-
www.buitwenverwachting.co.za *Mon-Sat 1200-3130, 1900-2100.
Map 1, D3, p246* The main restaurant serves a cosmopolitan
menu with flawless Italian, French and South African dishes. Good
service, upmarket, prices reflect the quality of the food.

Catharina's, Steenberg Country Hotel, Spaanschemat River
Rd, Constantia, **T** 021-7132222. *0700-2130. Map 1, D3, p246*
The principal restaurant in a 5-star hotel. Breakfast is served in
the conservatory, lunch and dinner under the oaks or at tables
set in cosy alcoves created from old wine vats. An elegant hotel
restaurant serving a mix of light snacks and excellent South African
fare such as West Coast mussels, Knynsa oysters and springbok loin
on polenta. Fine wine list.

♜♜♜ **La Colombe**, Constantia Uitsig, Constantia, **T** 021-7942390, lacolombe.co.za *1200-1500, 1830-2200, closed July and Aug.* *Map 1, D3, p246* Excellent French menu with strong Provençal flavours. Delicious fresh fish and a range of meat and duck dishes, with an emphasis on rich sauces. During fine weather you can sit outside and look over the gardens and a pool.

♜♜♜ **The Greenhouse**, The Cellars-Hohenort Hotel, 93 Brommersvlei Rd, Constantia, **T** 021-7942137, www.cellars-hohenort.com *0730-2200. Map 1, D3, p246* One of 2 highly rated restaurants at this 5-star hotel, set in a pretty conservatory with white wicker furniture. The Michelin-trained chef produces top-quality fare – mostly modern South African, so expect fresh fish and game, and divine desserts. Excellent wine list to match. One of the finest restaurants in the area.

♜♜ **Barrister's Grill**, corner of Kildare and Main St, Newlands, **T** 021-6716907. *Mon-Sat 0800-2300, Sun 1700-2300. Map 1, C4, p246* Open daily from breakfast through to late evening. A popular steakhouse that has expanded into a trendy bistro/café during the day with plenty of alfresco tables. Still retains the Mock-Tudor timber decor of the steakhouse. Plenty for vegetarians.

♜♜ **Fiamma's**, 23-25 Wolf St, Wynberg, **T** 021-7616175. *Tue-Fri 1200-1500, also Mon-Sat 1800-2200. Map 1, D4, p246* Smart Italian restaurant serving fine traditional dishes such as home-made pasta and celebrated three-meat patties. Good vegetarian choices. Friendly service, attractive surrounds.

♜♜ **Silver Tree**, Kirstenbosch Botanical Gardens, **T** 021-7629585. *0800-2200. Map 1, D3, p246* Stunning setting at the foot of the gardens, with views up towards Table Mountain. Fairly pricey but good meals, including Cape specialities such as bobotie, plus salads, steaks and pasta. Friendly service.

¶ **Don Pedro's**, 113 Roodebloem Rd, Woodstock, **T** 021-4470482, info@donpedro.co.za *1900-late. Map 6, B7, p254* Informal, bustling restaurant serving huge portions of South African food, pasta and pizza at cheap prices. Very popular, focal point of the local community, great mixed crowd, book ahead. Recommended.

¶ **Hussar Grill**, 10 Main Rd, Rondebosch **T** 021-6899516. *1200-2200.* Cosy, old-fashioned steakhouse, extolled by locals for serving the best steaks in Cape Town. Wide choice including lots of game, but it's the standard beef that's the reason for coming here. Convivial atmosphere, retro-style booths, live music at weekends.

¶ **Pancho's**, Lower Main Rd, Observatory, **T** 021-4474854. *1200-2300. Map 7, A3, p255* Mexican dishes in a lively atmosphere, all the usual tacos and fajitas, good home-made nachos, big portions, nothing fancy but a fun place. Tasty cocktails – try the strawberry margarita.

Cafés

¶ **Marigolds**, 5 Grove Av, Claremont, **T** 021-6744670. *Mon-Fri 0830-1630, Sat 0830-1400. Map 1, C4, p246* One of the few vegetarian restaurants in town, good selection of quiche, baked potatoes, soups and salads. A self-proclaimed meat-free zone.

¶ **Nino's**, Cavendish Sq, Claremont, **T** 021-6837288. *Mon-Sat 0900-late, Sun 1000-1800. Map 1, C4, p246* Popular haunt for shoppers to rest up and try Nino's toasted paninis, salads or pasta.

¶ **Obz Café**, 115 Lower Main Rd, Observatory, **T** 021-4485555. *0730-late. Map 7, B3, p255* Popular Observatory haunt open all day for light meals, coffee or cocktails, great salads and sandwiches, also has main meals in the evenings and occasional live music.

False Bay

Restaurants

¶¶¶ **Bon Appetit**, 90 St George's St, Simon's Town,
T 021-7862412. *Tue-Sat 1200-1400, 1830-2200. Map 1, I3, p247*
One of the finest restaurants on the peninsula, specializing in
top-notch French cuisine – the chef is Michelin-trained. Excellent
set menus and imaginative main meals such as ravioli of rabbit
plus French staples like confit de canard. Be sure to book ahead.

¶¶ **Bertha's**, Quayside Centre, Wharf Rd, Simon's Town,
T 021-7862138. *0900-2300. Map 1, I3, p247* A seafood grill and
coffee house in the centre of town in a prime location overlooking
the yacht harbour. During the day the outside terrace is a good place
to enjoy good fresh seafood and watch the goings on in the harbour.
Inside is a dining area perfect for large family meals. Great selection
of fresh seafood dishes, good value. Recommended.

¶¶ **Black Marlin**, Miller's Point, 2 km from Simon's Town,
T 021-7861621, www.blackmarlin.co.za *1200-1600, 1800-2000,
lunch only on Sun. Map 1, I3, p247* Set in an old whaling station,
this place is well known for its excellent seafood and is a good
point to stop for lunch on the way to Cape Point. Fabulous sea
views and a wide range of fresh seafood, delicious crayfish and
kingclip skewers, also good-value evening menu. Great wine list.
Recommended, although it gets busy with tour buses in summer.

¶¶ **Cape to Cuba**, Main Rd, Kalk Bay, **T** 021-7881566. *1130-1600,
1800-1030. Map 1, G3, p247* Atmospheric Cuban restaurant and
cocktail bar serving good-value seafood with a Caribbean edge.
Great setting on the water's edge with tables overlooking the
harbour, funky decor, enjoyable Cuban music.

¶¶ **Penguin Point Café**, Boulders Beach, **T** 021-7861758, www.bouldersbeach.co.za *0730-late.* *Map 1, I3, p247* Open for breakfasts through to dinner. Excellent restaurant with bar and sundeck which is always busy with day-trippers. Good English breakfasts, cocktails (including the popular Pickled Penguins), and wide choice of mains, from mussel chowder and lamb brochetta to grilled catch-of-the-day or crayfish thermidore. Recommended.

¶¶ **Quarterdeck** , Jubilee Sq, Simon's Town, **T** 021-7863825. *0800-1900, Fri open until 2300.* *Map 1, I3, p247* Simple café with great views over the harbour, serving sandwiches, burgers and interesting salads like avocado with smoked chicken and biltong. Also has a Cape Malay buffet on Friday evenings.

¶¶ **Railway House**, Railway Station, Muizenberg, **T** 021-7883252. *Tues-Sat 1200-2200, Sun 1000-1600, 1800-late.* *Map 1, F4, p246* Chic restaurants in the historic railway building, subtle contemporary decor, fusion menu, good-value set menus, old-style dinner dances held on Friday evenings.

¶ **The Brass Bell**, by the railway station in Kalk Bay, **T** 021-7885455, *Mon-Fri 1200-1600, 1800-2300, Sat & Sun also 0800-1100, pub open throughout the day.* *Map 1, G3, p246* A well-known and very popular pub and restaurant in a great location right by the waves. Simple set-up serving pub meals and good pizzas and fish and chips. Downstairs gets packed with a young crowd, gets very busy around sunset, great for a cool beer outside close to the waves. More expensive restaurant upstairs serving fresh fish and grills.

¶ **Café Pescado**, 118 St George's St (opposite Jubilee Square), Simon's Town, **T** 021-7862272. *1200-2230.* *Map 1, I3, p247* A popular family set-up serving some simple, delicious seafood. Try the calamari and always check what the catch of the day is.

Also has good sharing platters with tasters of the daily catch served with prawns. Also a popular bar with weekly live music. Recommended.

¶ **Empire Café**, 11 York Rd, Muizenberg, **T** 021-7881250. *Tues-Sun 0700-1600, Fri & Sat until 2100. Map 1, F4, p247* Hip new eatery serving eclectic breakfasts and lunchtime fare, including interesting salads and omelettes (try the famous bacon, banana and honey) and some seafood specials.

¶ **Gaylords**, 65 Main Rd, Muizenberg, **T** 021-7885470. *Wed-Sun 1200-1500, 1700-2100, Mon 1700-2100. Map 1, F3, p246* Unpretentious, bustling Indian restaurant set in an old Victorian cottage with tacky decorations and good-value, highly rated North and South Indian curries, recommended for seafood and vegetarian dishes.

¶ **Horatio's**, Lord Nelson Inn, Simon's Town, **T** 021-7861386. *1900-2200. Map 1, I3, p247* Pleasant hotel restaurant with blue walls and harbour views. Simple seafood specials and grills. Good value and friendly service.

¶ **Salty Sea Dog**, next to Quayside Centre, Simon's Town. **T** 021-7861918. *Mon-Sat 1000-2100, Sun 1000-1630. Map 1, I3, p247* Cheap and cheerful place serving fresh fish and chips with seats overlooking the harbour. Good value, friendly and swift service. Popular with groups.

¶ **The Timeless Way**, 106 Main Rd, Kalk Bay, **T/F** 021-7885619, kellyv@mweb.co.za, *1200-1600, 1800-2230, Sat & Sun from 0900. Map 1, G3, p246* An excellent, old-fashioned restaurant serving Cape cuisine, steaks and seafood. The bobotie is good, as is the fresh pasta. Ronnie and Kelly ensure a high standard of service.

Cafés

Ψ **Balmoral on Beach**, Beach Rd, Muizenberg, **T** 021-7886441. *0900-1700, closed Tue. Map 1, F4, p246* Don't be fooled by the grand name: this is little more than a friendly little café serving healthy breakfasts and surfer-friendly fry-ups as well as light lunches like butternut risotto cakes.

Ψ **Mediterraneo**, Quayside Centre, Simon's Town. *0800-1800. Map 1, I3, p247* Home-made soups, cakes and deli. Breezy setting, great for afternoon snacks.

Ψ **Olympia Café**, 138 Main Rd, Kalk Bay, **T** 021-7886396, olympia@my.co.za *0700-2100. Map 1, G3, p247* A Kalk Bay institution, this laid-back café serves the best bread on the Peninsula, plus light lunches, fabulous cakes and fresh daily specials. Great atmosphere and good service, but expect to queue at weekends. The bakery at the back turns into a restaurant and tiny theatre at night.

Around Cape Town

Hermanus and the Whale Coast

ΨΨΨ **The Burgundy**, 16 Harbour Rd, **T** 028-3122800. *0830-1615.* Restored rural cottage by the sea. One of the top restaurants in town but very relaxed and good value, with tables spilling onto a shady terrace outside. Excellent seafood including superb grilled crayfish.

ΨΨΨ **Seafood at the Marine**, The Marine, Marine Dr, **T** 028-3131000, www.collectionmcgrath.com *1200-1500, 1900-2200.* Voted the best seafood restaurant in South Africa in 2004, this superb restaurant serves the freshest seafood in stylish surrounds. The menu is refreshingly unfussy and short, and includes a crayfish platter, seafood bunny chow, 'Rich man's' fish and chips, and gorgeous prawn and leek ravioli with lobster bisque. The wine list is excellent and the service friendly and fast. Recommended.

♔♔ **Bientang's Cave**, Marine Drive, **T** 028-3123454, www.bientangscave.com *1130-1600, Fri & Sat 1900-2100.* The name doesn't lie – the venue is an actual cave with an extended deck overlooking the waves. Excellent seafood buffets and famous bouillabaisse soup, simple wood benches and long tables, very popular, book ahead. Access is via steps from the carpark on Marine Drive between the village square and *Marine Hotel* – look out for the Bientang Seaworld sign.

♔♔ **Mogg's Country Cookhouse**, **T** 028-3124321. *By appointment only. Lunches Wed-Sun, evening meals Fri and Sat only. Situated in the Hemel-en-Aarde Valley, 12 km from Hermanus centre. Take the R43 out of town for Cape Town, after 2 km turn onto the R320 for Caledon.* The restaurant is run by Jenny and her daughter, Julia, who prepare a seasonal menu. Every dish is freshly prepared and served in a lovely rustic setting. Recommended.

♔ **Ciro's**, Franken St, Gansbaai, T028-3841106. *Tues-Sat 1100-late, Sun 1100-1600.* Popular pub in a historic cottage, tiny interior or shady terrace outside, great seafood and steaks.

♔ **The Fish Shoppe**, Market Sq, **T** 028-3121819. *0730-1800.* Bait shop selling cheap and cheerful fish and chips and deep fried calamari, with tables on the pavement outside.

♔ **Fisherman's Cottage**, Market Sq, **T** 028-3123642. *Mon-Sat 1030-1530, 1815-2130, Sun 1030-1530.* Tiny place set in an old thatched cottage serving excellent seafood, simple dishes such as seafood potjie, charming setting. Choose a veranda table in good weather. Known as the smallest pub in town.

¶ **The Great White House**, 5 Geelbekstreet, T028-3833273, www.white-house.co.za Popular thatched house, large restaurant in courtyard popular with divers, good location close to the harbour.

¶ **Mariana's** , 12 Du Toit St, Stanford **T** 028-3410272. *0900-1600*. Deli stocked with local products, cheeses, stuffed olives and chutneys. Also serves bistro-style meals – the mussels are particularly good.

¶ **Ocean Basket**, Fashion Sq, Main Rd, **T** 028-3121529. *Mon-Fri 1200-2100, Sat 1200-2200, Sun 1200-2030*. The usual fresh, fried seafood you can expect from this chain. Good value, quick meals.

¶ **Prince of Whales**, Astoria Village, **T** 028-3130725. *Mon-Fri 0815-1700, Sat 0815-1330*. Excellent breakfasts, filled pancakes, sandwiches, cakes and fresh croissants.

¶ **Zebra Crossing**, Main Rd, **T** 028-3123906. *Mon-Sat 0900-0200, Sun 1000-0200*. Lively pub with zebra-print theme, serving burgers, steaks, salads and ploughman lunches. Turns into a popular drinking haunt later at night.

Stellenbosch

¶¶¶ **Governer's Hall**, Lanzerac Manor, **T** 021-8871132. *1200-1430, 1500-2200*. *Map 8, E2/3, p256* Main restaurant in this luxury hotel. Historic setting, informal lunches and formal dinners, high standards and corresponding prices, good wine list.

Grape expectations

South Africa has become one of the world's major wine producers, and although its wine industry is not yet as successful as that of Australia, standards are improving rapidly. A number of Cape wines are excellent and most are very good value.

The Cape's wine industry was started in earnest by Simon van der Stel in 1679. Previously, vines had been grown by Van Riebeeck in Company's Garden and in the area known today as the suburb of Wynberg. As the early settlers moved inland and farms were opened up in the sheltered valleys, more vines were planted.

Van der Stel produced the first quality wines on Constantia estate in Cape Town (see p65), but a great boost to the fledgling industry came with the arrival of the French Huguenots in 1688, and for a while the wines produced at Constantia were even in demand in France.

The industry received a further boost in 1806 when the English, at war with France, started to import South African wines. However, during the apartheid era the wine industry suffered, as sanctions hindered exports and the Kooperatieve Wijnbouwers Vereniging (KWV) controlled both prices and production quotas. The KWV has since lost much of its power, allowing the industry to experiment and expand.

The modern wine industry has developed out of the need to find better quality grapes. The Hanepoort grape proved to be too delicate to travel. These days, hundreds of varieties are cultivated in the Cape region. Each river valley produces its own distinct wine, using the grape best suited to the local climatic conditions. The area around Stellenbosch remains the heartland of the industry, but you are likely to see vines growing in the Cape wherever there is a guaranteed supply of irrigated water.

¶¶ The Coachman, Ryneveld St, next to Village Museum, T021-8832230. *1200-midnight.* Map 8, E2/3, p256 Cobbled courtyard with a beer garden feel, serving light meals and Cape specialities such as bobotie, springbok stew and lamb chops. Convenient location but can get busy with tour groups.

¶¶ Decameron, 50 Plein St, **T** 021-8833331. *1200-1430, 1800-1000, closed Sun evening.* Map 8, E2/3, p256 Long-standing Italian favourite with a relaxing beer garden shaded by vines. The wood-fired pizzas and fresh pasta are delicious, and there's also a choice of reliable, traditional Italian mains.

¶¶ De Volkskombuis, Old Strand Rd, **T** 021-8872121, www.volkskombuis.co.za *1200-2100, closed Sun eve.* Map 8, E2/3, p256 Well-known for its traditional South African fare, with a good choice from around the country. Try the Karoo lamb or home-made springbok pies. Professional service, atmospheric thanks to the setting in a restored Herbert Baker Cape Dutch homestead, with views across the Eerste River. A sensibly priced treat.

¶¶ Fishmonger, Sanlam Bldg, c/o Plein and Ryneveld sts, **T** 021-8877835, fishmonger@adept.co.za *Mon-Sat 1200-1000, Sun 1200-2100.* Map 8, E2/3, p256 Portuguese-style seafood restaurant serving a great choice of fresh Cape seafood – kingclip, calamari, tiger prawns and the like – including taster platters for those who can't decide. Also has a sushi chef, and a choice of vegetarian dishes. Good service, booking essential. Recommended.

¶¶ Stellenbosch Hotel, 162 Dorp St, T021-8873644, stb-hotel@mweb.co.za *0700-2200.* Map 8, E2/3, p256 Part of the hotel and well-known for its game dishes. Just about everything from the African bush is served up, from crocodile kebabs and kudu steaks, to zebra or giraffe loin. Also has specials like ostrich cottage pie or warthog ribs, plus some seafood.

¶ **Blue Orange**, Dorp St, **T** 021-8872052. *Mon-Sat 0800-1800, Sun 0830-1700. Map 8, E2/3, p256* Delicious range of breakfasts, good-value snacks and sandwiches plus light lunches such as quiche and pasta. Interesting mix of students, well-coifed locals and backpackers. Also has an attached deli selling local produce such as jams, bread, fruit and veg.

¶ **Café Nouveau**, cnr Plein and Ryneveld Sts, **T** 021-8875627. *Mon-Fri 0700-2200, Sat 0730-2200, Sun 0830-2200. Map 8, E2/3, p256* Lovely Austrian-style café with gilt-edged mirrors and tightly packed tables serving sandwiches, coffee and cakes, as well as robust Germanic dishes like Bratwurst with fried potatoes.

¶ **Dros**, corner of Bird and Alexander sts, **T** 021-8864856. *0800-midnight. Map 8, E2/3, p256* A large bar-cum-restaurant with plenty of outdoor seating in a lively square. Popular chain serving standard pub fare such as burgers, steaks and pizza. Good value, but portions are on the small side.

¶ **Ha!Ha!**, Ryneveld St, opposite Village Museum. **T** 021-8871592. *Mon-Sat 0800-late.   Map 8, E2/3, p256* Bustling, vibey café-bar serving light meals, pasta, salads and steaks. Good place to stop for a cool drink or coffee and cake after visiting the Village Museum. Turns into a popular bar in the evening.

¶ **Leathers**, cnr Church and Rynevled Sts, **T** 021-8829415. *0800-1900. Map 8, E2/3, p256* New, stylish bistro (coupled, oddly, with a leatherwares shop) with cool, tiled interior and pleasant terrace garden, serving light meals and snacks. Nice place to enjoy an early-evening glass of wine.

¶ **Mexican Kitchen**, 25 Bird St, **T** 021-8829997, www.mexicankitchen.co.za *1100-midnight. Map 8, E2/3, p256* Lively cantina-style restaurant serving huge portions of nachos, bean soup, fajitas, tacos and steaks. Relaxed setting with inventive decor – some of the seats are swings. Also hosts salsa sessions and serves good shooters and cocktails. Recommended.

♦ **Spice Café**, 17 Krige St, **T** 021-8838480. *Mon-Sat 0800-1800, Sun 1000-1400*. *Map 8, E2/3, p256* Colourful café serving milkshakes, open sandwiches, daily salad specials and fabulous cakes such as the towering Millionaire's cake. Also hosts occasional live music.

Franschhoek

♦♦♦ **Le Ballon Rouge**, 12 Reservoir St, **T** 021-8762651, www.ballon-rouge.co.za *0815-2200*. *Map 8, E6, p256* Part of the guesthouse. Well-known restaurant set in bright dining room and shady courtyard serving unusual and eccentric South African dishes. Examples include fried four-cheese cannelloni or frozen chicken liver pate with beetroot cream, and roast springbok topped with sweet potato ice cream. Be prepared for strange mixes of sweet and savoury, cold and hot. Also has award-winning wine list.

♦♦♦ **La Couronne**, Robertsvlei Rd, **T** 021-8762770, www.lacouronnehotel.co.za *0800-2100*. *Map 8, E6, p256* Small, formal restaurant based at the ultra-smart Couronne Hotel and wine estate. Perfect setting overlooking the vineyards, good menu with separate vegetarian section, light lunches are proving popular, also arranges picnics and offers 5-course dinners. Long wine list.

♦♦♦ **Le Quartier Français**, 16 Huguenot Rd, **T** 021-8762151, www.lequartier.co.za *1200-1400, 1900-2300*. *Map 8, E6, p256* Rated as one of the best restaurants in the Western Cape. Expensive French and South African dishes, rather fussy and over-rated, but nevertheless a nice place for a treat.

🍴 **The Grapevine**, Huguenot Rd, **T** 021-8762520. *0800-2100. Map 8, E6, p256* Family restaurant serving big breakfasts, light lunches (try the tasty butternut soup) and game braais in the evening. Also serves some good Cape Malay dishes like the ever-popular bobotie.

🍴 **Le Bon Vivant**, 66 Huguenot Rd, **T** 021-8762717, lebonvivant@mweb.co.za *0800-2100. Map 8, E6, p256* Small garden restaurant with tables set in dappled shade, serving delicious light lunches (don't miss the local smoked trout sandwich) and a five-course dinner which has had excellent reports. Good value, friendly service. Recommended.

🍴 **La Maison de Chamonix**, 1 Uitkyk St, **T** 021-8762393. *1100-1500, 1800-late, closed Mon. Map 8, E6, p256* Highly rated upmarket country-style restaurant set on a wine estate (see below). Fine selection of South African and international dishes including a vegetarian menu. Better equipped than most to take families, with an on-site jungle gym and children's menu.

🍴 **Monneaux**, Franschhoek Country House, Main Rd, **T** 021-8763386 www.fch.co.za. *1230-1430, 1830-2200. Map 8, E6, p256* Contemporary fusion cuisine, attractive outdoor terrace and cosy dining room. Lots of game and fish with strong spicing, such as quail with harissa or trout and tapenade. Good local wine list.

🍴 **La Petite Fêrme**, Pass Rd, 2 km out of town, **T** 021- lapetite@iafrica.com *1200-1600. Map 8, E6, p256* Spectacular views over the Franschhoek valley from this smart country hotel and 'boutique' winery. The restaurant is well known for its wholesome country fare as well as delicate fusion dishes like smoked salmon on sweet potato and coconut mash, or hearty French cassoulet. Good desserts and wine list, too.

❢ **Bijoux**, 58 Huguenot Rd, **T** 021-8763474. *Tue-Sun 1100-2200 Map 8, E6, p256* Relaxed bistro with a pleasant garden setting serving well-prepared grills such as rack of lamb, as well as local smoked rainbow trout and vegetable tempura. Very popular as a lunch spot.

❢ **The French Connection**, corner Bordeaux and Huguenot Rds, **T** 021-8764056. *1200-2100. Map 8, E6, p256* French bistro serving refreshingly un-fussy food such as steamed mussels, steak-frites or Toulouse sausages and mash. Kids have their own menu. Pleasant bustling atmosphere.

Paarl

❢❢❢ **Bosman's**, Grande Roche Hotel, Plantasie St, **T** 021-8632727, www.grandroche.com *0700-1000, 1200-2100. Map 8, B4, p256* Award-winning international cuisine of the highest standard in a grand vineyard-fringed setting. Popular three-course set lunch, but the real treat is the celebrated five-course 'Flavours of the Cape' menu (R450), offering superbly created examples of Cape cuisine. Good choice of vegetarian dishes, award-winning wine list. Regarded as one of the finest (and most expensive) restaurants in South Africa, and now with Relais Gourmand status.

❢❢❢ **Laborie**, Taillefert St, **T** 021-8073095 *0900-1600. Map 8, C4, p256* Restaurant on the wine estate with pleasant seating under trees. Delicious Cape and Mediterranean dishes, lots of contemporary choices like tea-smoked chicken and apple salad, also some vegetarian options. Smart but relaxed atmosphere, good service. Recommended.

❢❢ **Boschendal**, Pniel Rd, **T** 021-8704211, www.boschedalwines.co.za *Lunch 1230-1500, café 1000-1700. Map 8, B4, p256* Picnic hampers in a lovely rural setting on this top wine estate, from November to April. Also a café and popular restaurant serving a cellar buffet. The vegetarian menu is exceptionally good for the country. The manor house was once the home of Cecil Rhodes.

ΨΨ **De Malle Madonna**, 127 Main Rd, **T** 0-8633925. *Tues-Sun 0830-1730* *Map 8, B4, p256* Cool and kooky café serving creamy quiches, huge sandwiches, burgers and wraps, plus towering cakes and muffins in the afternoon. Refreshingly modern spot for a snack.

ΨΨ **Kontreihuis**, 193 Main St (in *Zomerlust* guesthouse), **T** 021-8722117. *1200-1500, 1830-2200.* *Map 8, B4, p256* Traditional Cape meals served in an attractive dining room, the sort of place where you are liable to linger after enjoying your meal.

ΨΨ **Pontac**, 16 Zion St (in *Pontac* guesthouse), **T** 021-8720460, www.pontac.com *1200-2100.* *Map 8, B4, p256* Informal and friendly restaurant in a cosy setting, serving traditional dishes (lots of game) plus weekly specials and imaginative vegetarian options. Good service.

ΨΨ **Rhebokskloof**, Rhebokskloof Estate, **T** 021-8638606, www.rhebokskloof.co.za *0800-1700, Thurs-Mon also for dinner.* *Map 8, B4, p256* Wonderful views from the terrace, where light lunches are served. Old fashioned interior is the setting for a heavier international evening menu. The club sandwiches and salads are good, as is the Sunday starter buffet. Also open for afternoon tea.

ΨΨ **Wagon Wheels**, 57 Lady Grey St, **T** 021-8725265. *Tues-Fri 1200-1400, 1800-2100, also Sat 1800-2200.* *Map 8, B4, p256* Deservedly famous upmarket steakhouse serving superb pepper and mustard steaks (meat is aged for four weeks), plus game in season and weekly fish specials.

¶ **Dros**, Main Rd, **T** 021-8630350. *0900-late.* Map 8, B4, p256
Outlet of pub-style chain serving steaks, ribs and pasta dishes in a
cellar atmosphere. Also has a good choice of beers at the bar.

¶ **Kosinrichting**, 19 Pastorie Av, **T** 021-8711353. *Mon-Sat
0800-1700. Map 8, B4, p256* Coffee shop serving light meals,
sandwiches and coffee and cakes, tables in the dappled shade of
oak trees.

Cape Town's nightlife scene is following hotly on the heels of Johannesburg, as a city renowned for its cutting-edge bars and clubs. Although nightlife in the Mother City is fairly laid back, it's easy to find a buzzing bar or live music on just about any night of the week. Saturday nights are the biggest, followed closely by Wednesdays, known as 'mini-Saturday' to Capetonians.

While bars are always free to get in, clubs usually charge an entry fee – generally from about R20 up to R60. In typical Cape Town style, opening hours are far from strict and you'll be hard pressed to find a place which closes before you're ready to call it a night. Bars tend to fill up from around 1800, while clubs are virtually deserted before midnight, and techno clubs stay open until well into the next morning. Some bars become clubs as the night progresses, so always check out both sets of listings.

Long Street is one of the main areas and is lined with bars, cafés and small clubs, popular with backpackers and fashionable, young locals. The main gay scene is at Green Point where there are great bars and clubs along the main road (see also p165). Observatory is the city's alternative hub, with laid-back bars and cafés.

Music is central to a night out and people get quite passionate about their tunes. You'll mostly hear mainstream house, but hip-hop and techno are popular, as are drum 'n' bass and Latin sounds. You should also hear Kwaito, a relaxed form of house with booming bass – the dance music from young, black Jo'burg. Kwaito is the biggest movement in music at the moment, although home-grown rock is more popular with young white people. There are a number of large-scale events held in and around Cape Town – popular nights include Vortex and Alien Safari – pure techno. Look out for flyers in bars and cafés. *The Cape Times* and *Argus* have good listings sections, as does *Cape Review* magazine. Otherwise, check out www.clubbersguide.co.za

The city centre

Bars

Drum Café, 32 Glyn St, Gardens, **T** 021-4611305, www.drumcafe.co.za *Mon, Wed, Fri & Sat 1800-2300 Map 2, D8, p249* Huge bar and live drumming venue serving light meals and featuring communal drumming sessions. Grab a drum and join in, or watch the professionals on Fri and Sat nights.

Jo'burg, 218 Long St, **T** 021-4220142. *Daily 1500-0300. Map 2, B6, p248* Trendy bar serving pints and cocktails to a mixed crowd, gay-friendly, relaxed during the week but gets very busy at weekends when DJs spin funky house and drum 'n' bass. One of the best in the area.

Kennedy's Cigar Bar, 251 Long St, **T** 021-4241212. *Daily 1200-late. Map 2, B6, p248* Upmarket cigar and cocktail lounge, old-fashioned brass-and-wood decor, daily live jazz, mature well-heeled crowd. Restaurant downstairs.

Mama Africa, 178 Long St, **T** 021-4248634. *Mon-Sat 1900-late. R10, free if you're eating. Map 2, B6, p248* Great live music every night, usually Marimba. Part of the popular restaurant, the bar is smallish with a long, wood-carved green mamba making up the bar. Limited seating, great atmosphere, quite touristy.

Perseverance Tavern, 83 Buitenkant St, **T** 021-4612440. *Daily from lunch-late. Map 2, D8, p249* Cape Town's oldest pub, pub food available in two dining rooms, beer garden, plenty of drinking corners, full on at the weekend, good Sunday roast lunch, live music.

Poo Na Na Souk Bar, Heritage Sq, 100 Shortmarket St, **T** 021-4234889. *Mon-Fri 1100-0130, Sat & Sun 1800-0130 Map 3, H10, p251* Ultra-trendy bar decked out in Moroccan lanterns and expensive fabrics, lovely balconies overlooking the even trendier *Moja* restaurant, usually relaxed atmosphere but sometimes host big-name international DJs.

Purple Turtle Pub, Long St, **T** 021-4236194. *Daily 1100-late. Map 2, A7, p249* Grotty pub which remains very popular, with a large, dark interior dotted with TV screens. Pub lunches, pool tables, live rock bands on Sat. *Virtual Turtle* is their internet café spin-off, upstairs.

Rafiki's, 13 Kloof Nek Rd, Gardens, **T** 021-4264731. *Daily 1100-late. Map 2, D4, p248* Popular bar overlooking Kloof Nek with a huge wrap-around balcony perfect for a sundowner. Occasional live music and braai evenings.

★ Up-for-it venues

Clubs

169, 169 Long St, **T** 021-4261107. *Thu, Fri and Sat 1900-late. R20. Map 2, B7, p249* R&B club with a lively, mixed crowd, some Kwaito. Fairly small venue, with a great balcony overlooking busy Long Street. Gets packed on Fridays.

Deluxe, cnr Longmarket and Long Sts, **T** 021-4224832. *Wed, Fri & Sat 2200-0400. Map 2, A7, p249* Popular new nightclub in the centre of town, cosy seating areas, large dance floor, well-known for its deep house, VIP room is a good party venue.

Dharma Club, 68 Kloof St, Gardens, **T** 021-4220909, www.the dharmaclub.com *1800-2300. Map 2, D4, p248* Small, trendy bar with vaguely Asian decor. Intimate setting and excellent music mixed by a live DJ, live music on Wednesdays, good fusion meals, but an over-dressed, pretentious crowd.

The Fez, 38 Hout St, **T** 021-4231456, www.fez.co.za *Tues-Sun 2200-late. R40. Map 2 ,A8, p249* Moroccan-themed interior, young and well-heeled crowd, funky house and themed parties.

The Lounge, 194 Long St. *Wed, Fri & Sat 2100-0200. Map 2, B6, p248* This fashionable bar and club incorporates several small rooms with big sofas. House music plays most nights, plus drum 'n' bass on Wednesdays. It also has a great balcony overlooking Long Street.

Mercury Live & Lounge, 43 de Villiers St, **T** 021-4652106, www.mercuryl.co.za *Mon, Wed-Fri 2100-late. Map 2, E10, p249*
Live music venue and club nights, rock and hip-hop acts play regularly, also holds weekly hip-hop parties and 'nostalgia' alternative rock nights. Popular venue, lively, young crowd.

Rhodes House, 60 Queen Victoria St, Gardens, **T** 021-4248844, www.rhodeshouse.com *Thur-Sat 2100-late. Map 2, E10, p249*
Rated as one of the best nightclubs in the city. Swanky lounge with dancefloor and al fresco courtyard, super-trendy decor, frequented by models and local celebs. Good music, fantastic but pricey drinks.

Sutra, 86 Loop St, **T** 021-4244218. *Wed-Sat 2100-0400. Map 2, A7, p249* 'Retro-East' styled bar and club, dancefloor on first floor, cocktail waitresses do the rounds downstairs, mix of hip-hop, deep house and Afro-Caribbean music. Free entry before 2300.

Vacca Matta, Seeff House, Foreshore, **T** 021-9101855.
2100-late. Full-on drinking haunt and cramped club with waitresses dancing on the bar, 'ladies' get in cheap and often get free cocktails, seriously tacky but resolutely popular.

Victoria and Alfred Waterfront

Bars

Den Anker, Victoria & Alfred Pierhead, **T** 021-4190249, www.denanker.co.za *Daily 0900-2300. Map 3, C11, p251* Belgian restaurant and bar specializing in a range of Belgian draught and bottled beers.

Ferryman's Tavern, next to the amphitheatre, Waterfront, **T** 021-4197748. *Daily 1100-2300. Map 3, C10, p251* A popular haunt with restaurant upstairs, outside seating, TV continually showing sports action, the olives and feta go well with the Mitchell's Beer brewed on site, a low-key crowd.

Quay Four, **T** 021-4192008. *Daily 1100-midnight. Map 3, B11, p251* Large shady deck overlooking the water, popular with well-heeled locals and tourists, good meals and great draught beer, one of the more pleasant pubs on the Waterfront.

Sports Café, Victoria Wharf, **T** 021-4195558. *Daily 1100-late. Map 3, B11, p251* Sports bar showing matches on big screens, rowdy atmosphere and a mostly white, rugby-playing clientele. American-style snacks and meals served.

Clubs

Cantina Tequila, Quay 5, Victoria Wharf, **T** 021-4190207, www.cantinatequila.com *Daily, 1100-late. Map 3, B11, p251* This Mexican restaurant transforms into a packed nightclub after about 2300, mostly chart music, popular with tourists.

Atlantic Seaboard

Bars

Bosa Nova, Somerset Rd, Green Point, **T** 021-250295. *Tues-Sat 2000-0200. Map 3, F10, p251* Large bar with seats overlooking the street, vague tropical theme, small dancefloor at the back, pop and house music.

Buddha Bar, Main Rd, Green Point, **T** 021-4344010. www.buddhabar.co.za *Closed Sun. Map 3, D8, p251* Sophisticated bar with balcony overlooking the action on Main Rd, Green Point, tastefully decorated in a subdued Asian feel, long bar with full range of imported drinks, excessively trendy for the media and model crowd, Wednesday is the big night out. Recommended for drinking and conversation whilst still keeping intact eardrums. Entry R20 after 2100.

Buena Vista Social Café, Main Rd, Green Point, **T** 021-4330611. *1200-late. Map 3, D7, p251* Cuban-themed bar and restaurant catering to a well-heeled crowd. Latin music, live bands at weekend, tasteful decor and a relaxed atmosphere, nice balcony, great spot for sophisticated cocktails on a hot evening.

Café Caprice, Victoria Rd, Camps Bay, **T** 021-4388315. *0900-late. Map 5, E4, p253* Popular café and bar with outdoor seats overlooking the beach, great fresh-fruit cocktails, beautiful, well-heeled crowd, gets packed at sunset.

Dizzy Jazz Café, 41 The Drive, Camps Bay, **T** 021-4382686. *Daily, 1200-0100. Map 5, E4, p253* Busy bar and live music venue, popular jazz nights at the weekend, wide terrace with sea views.

Eclipse, Victoria Rd, Camps Bay, **T** 021-4380882. *1730-late. Map 5, E3, p253* London-owned lounge bar overlooking the beach, minimalist interior, fashionable place to be seen at sunset, great but relatively pricey cocktails.

La Med, Glen Country Club, Victoria Rd, Clifton, **T** 021-4385600, www.lamed.co.za *1100-late. Map 5, off 2H, p253* A Cape Town institution: hugely popular, with a busy bar overlooking the sea and good pub food. It's great for a sundowner, but you'll be hard pressed to find a seat. Turns into a raucous club later on.

Sandbar, Victoria Rd, Camps Bay, **T** 021-4388336. *Tue-Sun, 1100-2300. Map 5, D4, p253* Popular for sundowners, café serving light meals during the day, shady tables on the pavement opposite the beach.

Tank, Cape Quater, Dixon Street, Green Point, **T** 021-4190007, www.the-tank.co.za *1100-late. Map 3, G10, p251* Showy but hugely popular bar and restaurant, white cube seats surround low tables, large tropical fish tank is the centrepiece. Hair-flicking models and body-builders will feel at home.

Tuscany Beach Café, 41 Victoria Rd, Camps Bay, **T** 021-4381213. *Daily 1100-2300. Map 5, E3, p253* Restaurant and bar with beach views, gets packed at sunset with cocktail-quaffing locals.

Clubs

The Bronx, 35 Somerset Rd, corner Napier St, Green Point, **T** 021-4212779, www.bronx.co.za *Daily 2000-late. Map 3, F10, p251* Cape Town's best-known and most popular gay bar and club, gets packed out at weekends, mostly men but women welcome, live DJs spin out thumping techno every night, karaoke on Mon.

Chilli 'n' Lime, 23 Somerset Rd, Green Point, **T** 083-9734673. *Wed, Fri & Sat 2000-0400. Map 3, F10, p251* Trendy bar and club spread over two floors, with mirrored walls, stylish lighting and a tiny dancefloor. Over-priced and very young, but playing good hip-hop on Saturday nights.

Purgatory, Dixon St, Green Point, **T** 021-4217464. *Wed, Fri & Sat 2200-0400. Map 3, G10, p251* Trumpeted as a 'model's' club, this is a stylish dance venue peopled by the young and beautiful. House music, leather sofas, cocktails – and models get in free.

Sliver, 27 Somerset Rd, Green Point Dixon St, **T** 021-4215798. *Map 3, F10, p251*   Trendy lounge bar, mostly gay clientele but also very popular with a style-conscious mixed crowd. Relaxed atmosphere, heats up later at night.

Southern Suburbs

Bars

Café Ganesh, Trill Rd, Observatory, **T** 021-4483435. *1200-0100. Map 7, A4, p255*   Lively little café and bar serving hearty Cape dishes and ice-cold beers in a leafy courtyard leading to a characterful interior. Very friendly, great place to meet local characters.

Forrester's Arms, Newlands Av, **T** 021-6895949. *Daily 1100-late. Map 7, F4, p255*   A favourite with students, especially sports jocks. Standard pub with a fun-loving, boozy scene.

The Green Man, Main Rd, Claremont. *Daily 1100-late. Map 1, C4, p246*   Most popular bar in Claremont despite its grim, modern interior. Very young, pint-downing crowd, small dancing area, mostly rock music, often frequented by Springbok players.

Keg & Grouse, Riverside Centre, Rondebosch, **T** 021-6893000. *Daily 1100-late. Map 1, C4, p246*   English-style pub serving bar meals, popular with local students and older sporty types.

Sports Café, Atrium Centre, Claremont, **T** 021-6741152. *1100-late. Map 1, C4, p246*   Popular second-floor bar showing all the important games on big screen TVs, tacky, busy balcony.

A Touch of Madness, Pepper Tree Sq, Nuttal Rd, Observatory, **T** 021-4482266. *Daily 1900-2300. Map 7, B4, p255*   Flamboyant bar with series of rooms decked out with tongue-in-cheek opulence, eccentric regulars, great atmosphere, good light meals.

Clubs

Gandalf's , 299 Lower Main Rd, Observatory, **T** 083-3300700. *Daily 2100-late Map 7, A3, p255* Vaguely Lord of the Rings-themed club, with large dance floor, 2 bars, mostly rock and nu metal, very young part-goth-part-surfer crowd, big with the UCT students. Has an edgier gothic room upstairs.

Independent Armchair Theatre, 135 Lower Main Rd, Observatory, **T** 021-4471514. *Daily 2000-0100. Map 7, A3, p255* Popular small-scale venue with huge sofas to lounge in, featuring films on Monday, jazz on Thursday, live bands most nights, excellent stand-up comedy from the Cape Comedy Collective on Sunday. Recommended.

False Bay

Bars

The Brass Bell, by the train station in Kalk Bay, **T** 021-7882943. *Daily 1100-late. Map 1, G3, p247* Celebrated Kalk Bay pub set right on the waves, great spot for a cold beer watching the sunset. Young, noisy crowd. Live music at weekends.

Cape to Cuba, Main Rd, Kalk Bay, **T** 021-7883695. *Tue-Sat, 1200-2300. Map 1, G3, p247* Atmospheric Cuban restaurant which turns into a cocktail bar later on, great drinks, lovely tables looking across the harbour, the Cuban music makes a nice change from the usual rock or house.

The Two and Sixpence, Main Rd, Simon's Town, next to *British Hotel*, **T** 021-7861371. *1000-midnight. Map 1, I3, p247* Local pub serving standard bar food, has pool tables and occasional live music. Friendly place for a pint.

Wipeout Bar, corner Camp and Main rds, Muizenberg, **T** 021-7884803. *Daily 1700-late. Map 1 F4, p246* Large tropical-themed bar, popular with backpackers and surfers, pub food, lurid cocktails, live music at weekends.

Stellenbosch

Bars and clubs

Bohemia Pub, Ryneveld St, **T** 021-8828375, www.bohemia.co.za *1000-late. Map 8, F2/3, p256* One of the main student haunts with an eccentric brightly-coloured interior and attractive wrap-around veranda. Gets very busy with a young clientele who come for the cold beers, relaxed atmosphere and occasional live music.

Dros, corner of Bird and Alexander sts, **T** 021-8864856. *0800-midnight. Map 8, E2/3, p256* The restaurant turns into a noisy bar late at night. Seats spill out onto the square. Backpackers' and students' favourite.

Fandango, 25 Bird St, **T** 021-8877506, info@fandango.co.za *9000-0100. Map 8, E2/3, p256* Café and bar offering internet access with tables spilling onto the square which are popular for after-work cocktails.

Mexican Kitchen, 25 Bird St, **T** 021-8829997, www.mexicankitchen.co.za *1100-midnight*. *Map 8, E2/3, p256* Lively Mexican cantina with weekly salsa sessions, gaudy cocktail and shooter specials. Women get a free cocktail on Tuesday nights.

Nu Bar, 51 Plein St, **T** 021-8868998. *Mon-Sat 1700-0300*. *Map 8, E2/3, p256* Crowded bar and club with tiny dance floor, DJ every night spinning hip-hop and house tunes to a young crowd. Popular party place.

Stones, Bird St, **T** 021-8871273. *1100-late*. *Map 8, E2/3, p256* Lively bar and pool hall, plenty of tables, seats on outdoor balcony overlooking the street, very popular, gets packed and noisy later in the night.

The Terrace, The Terrace, Alexander St, **T** 021-3871942. *1200-1500, 1830-late*. *Map 8, E2/3, p256* Busy pub with a vaguely Irish theme. Offers outdoor tables overlooking the Braak and live music most nights.

Tollie's, Drostdy Centre, Plein St, **T** 021-8839747. *2100-late*. *Map 8, E2/3, p256* Popular nightclub, gets packed with students on weekend nights, dance and pop music, occasional live bands.

South Africa is the only place
in the world where a revolution
has been made to the accompaniment
of four-part harmonies

Abdullah Ibrahim
The pianist, popularly known as Dollar Brand,
arguably the godfather of Cape Jazz

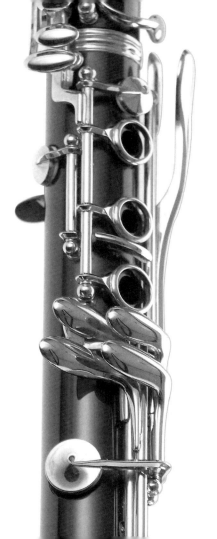

Following fast in Jo'Burg's footsteps, Cape Town is gaining a solid reputation for having a vibrant arts scene. Music, as always, is the cultural focal point, with live music – particularly jazz – remaining hugely popular and culminating in the yearly North Sea Jazz Festival, see also p183. The comedy circuit, too, is booming, attracting talent from around South Africa and overseas. The city also prides itself on its well-established classical music, opera and dance companies, although these have been radically modernized in the last decade – the staid, whites-only scene is becoming far more inclusive and experimental (and therefore much more interesting). Modern dance and theatre are popular, although much of the fodder for political theatre, once the most fertile genre in the performing arts, has disappeared. Instead, large-scale musicals have become the most popular productions.

Computicket: www.computicket.com, T 083-9158000, www.computicket.co.za, sells tickets for nationwide theatre, concerts and sport events.

Cinema

Cape Town recently launched the annual **Cape Town World Cinema Festival**, to be held every year in November, and there is an annual gay and lesbian film festival, known as the **Out in Africa** festival, held every year in March-April. Despite Cape Town's major role as a film location – the city and its surrounds have acted as stand-ins for an impressive range of movies in recent years – there is little in the way of local cinema. An exception is the films by Leon Schuster, South Africa's best-known slap-stick comic director and actor, despised by critics but responsible for the country's highest earning films. He plays on South African insecurities and comments on political currents through the unlikely medium of toilet gags and stereotyping.

You can catch the latest Schuster movie, as well as international releases, at the two major cinema groups, **Nu Metro** and **Ster-Kinekor**, both of which have several modern multiplexes dotted around the city. Some of the Ster-Kinekor multiplexes (V & A Waterfront and Cavendish Square) have an attached Cinema Nouveau, screening foreign and art-house cinema. There are also a couple of independent cinemas which screen international and art-house releases. New films are released on Friday. Evening and weekend shows are very popular so booking ahead is a good idea. You'll have to do this in person, as the cinema phone lines do not accept foreign credit cards. Daily newspapers have full listings.

Imax cinema, in the BMW Pavilion at the V & A Waterfront, **T** 021-4197365, www.imax.co.za *Map 3, B10, p251* Shows special format films on a giant screen with 'six-channel wrap-around digital sound'. Check the papers for listings of what's on. Tickets cost approximately R50 for adults and each film lasts for one hour.

Labia, 68 Orange St, Gardens, **T** 021-4245927, www.labia.co.za, *R30-60*. *Map 2, D5, p248* This is perhaps Cape Town's most enjoyable cinema, showing independent international films and with a café serving good pre-movie snacks. It is licensed, so you can take your glass of wine into the movie.

Nu Metro, www.numetro.co.za, V & A Waterfront. *Map 3, B11, p251* 11 screens, about R20-25, large, modern complex, roomy air-conditioned cinemas, block-busters and new releases; also has branches at Century City and in Claremont *Map 1, C4, p246*. Tickets are half-price on Tuesdays.

Ster-Kinekor, www.sterkinekor.com, Golden Acre, Adderley St. *Map 2, A9, p249* Usual multiplex set-up, most shows get sold out on Fridays and Saturdays . Also has branches in Kenilworth and Cavendish Square mall *Map 3, H11, p251*

Comedy

The comedy circuit is booming in Cape Town, led by the **Cape Comedy Collective**, a group of comedians who tour the city hosting nights at different venues. The scene is pretty edgy, playing on the profusion of sensitive issues that plague modern South Africa – not for the easily offended. It is also a fairly mixed scene, certainly in terms of the comedians themselves, although audiences tend to be mostly white. Comedians come and go at break-neck speed, but some of the most popular at time of writing include well-established Mark Banks and David Kau. Stand-up shows, the best of which are on weekends (including Sunday night) are usually of a high standard, offering a hilarious and thought-provoking insight to the city – providing not too many of the punch lines are in Afrikaans. For listings and information check the *Cape Times* or visit www.comedyclub.co.za

Bijou, Lower Main Rd, Observatory, **T** 021-4480183. *Tue-Sun 2000-late*. *Map 7, A3, p255* Ultra-fashionable club/bar/open-air theatre. Hosts some of the stand-up comedians visiting Cape Town for the annual Smirnoff Comedy Festival, held in October.

Comedy Warehouse, 55 Somerset Rd, Green Point, **T** 021-4252175. *2000-late. Map 3, F10, 251* Stand-up comedy on Friday and Saturday, also hosts Smirnoff Sessions and Cape Comedy Collective.

Independent Armchair Theatre, 135 Lower Main Rd, Observatory, **T** 021-4471514. *Daily 2000-0100. Map 7, A3, p255* Popular venue with huge sofas to lounge in, hosts the Cape Comedy Collective on Sunday, also sometimes has open mic nights.

Dance

The dance scene is not as big as one might expect, considering Cape Town's thriving arts scene, but there are occasionally one or two shows on that are worth seeing. Ballet is no longer prominent, but there is some interesting modern dance around, especially when it incorporates aspects of African dance. Tap-dancing, too, is making a bit of a comeback, although there's little here that can't be seen at home.

The Cape Town City Ballet, Cottage 3, Lover's Walk, Rosebank, www.capetowncityballet.org.za, **T** 021-6503527. *Map 7, H4, p255* This company has a long and illustrious history, starting with the establishment of Dulci Howes' UCT Ballet Company in 1934. Although once a large and well-funded company, it has suffered in recent years from the reallocation of government funding, and the regular large-scale, big-bucks productions have been replaced with a smaller company of just 22 dancers, with performances to recorded music instead of with an accompanying orchestra. Nevertheless, they remain of a high standard, concentrating on traditional favourites such as *Giselle* and *Cinderella*.

Jazzart, Artscape Theatre Centre, Foreshore, east of the train station, **T** 021-4109848, www.jazzart.co.za   The other major player in Cape Town's dance scene is the oldest modern dance company in South Africa, founded in 1975. Unlike the City Ballet, Jazzart was not granted funding during apartheid – little surprise considering its history of cultural involvement and multi-racial performances. The company continues to be actively involved in disadvantaged communities, working as a racially mixed group and creating a fusion of Western and African styles.

Music

Cape Jazz is perhaps the city's greatest cultural gift, and if you get the chance try and see some live acts while you're here. Jazz was, and remains, an important expression of cultural trends in modern South Africa, and Cape Town has produced some of its greatest exponents. The **North Sea Jazz Festival**, see p183, is held every May and attracts a glittering array of artists, including international acts like Elvis Costello, Jamie Cullum and Alicia Keys in 2004. See also p230.

Classical music and opera, although only recently moving away from the realm of the white and wealthy, is becoming increasingly accessible – not least at the summer concerts held on Sundays at the Kirstenbosch Botanical Gardens, not to be missed if you're here in summer. The **Cape Town Opera**, www.capetownopera.co.za, stages regular performances, with new up-and-coming singers leading the way. Cape Town also has a well-respected Philharmonic Orchestra, with concerts held at the Artscape Complex.

Rock and funk bands are big business, and are best caught at the Long Street or Obs Festivals – Just Jinger is the most popular and successful home-grown rock band at the moment.

The Brass Bell, Kalk Bay, **T** 021-7885455. *1200-late. Map 1, G3, p247* This long-term favourite has one of the best locations on False Bay, set just above the waves with views of the Atlantic.

The bar is nothing special, serving up cheap meals and beers to a young, surfer crowd, but it's a great setting for listening to live rock and funk bands. Live performances on Fri and Sat nights.

Dizzy Jazz Café, 41 The Drive, Camps Bay, **T** 021-4382686. *1700-late, closed Tue. Map 5, E4, p253* Busy bar and live jazz, intimate venue compared to others, friendly crowd, appealingly down-to-earth, good food served, very popular jazz nights from Thurs to Sun. Music starts at 2030.

Drum Café, 32 Glyn St, Gardens, **T** 021-4611305, www.drumcafe. co.za *2000-late. Map 2, D9, p249* Huge, popular bar featuring communal drumming sessions or professionals on Friday and Saturday nights.

Green Dolphin, V & A Waterfront, **T** 021-4217471, www.greendolphin.co.za. *1200-late. Map 3, C10, p251* Restaurant and jazz venue on the Waterfront featuring top local jazz groups that play while you eat.

Independent Armchair Theatre, 135 Lower Main Rd, Observatory, **T** 021-4471514. *2000-late. Map 7, A3, p255* Popular venue with huge sofas to lounge in, jazz on Thursday, live bands most nights.

Kirstenbosch Summer Concerts, Kirstenbosch Botanical Gardens, www.nbi.ac.za *Every Sun from 1700 Nov to Mar. Map 1, D3, p246* Idyllic setting, picnics on the lawns, concerts varying from folk and jazz to classical and opera.

Mama Africa, 178 Long St, **T** 021-4248634. *1900-late. Map 2, B7, p249* Great live music every night, usually Marimba.

Mercury Live & Lounge , 178 43 de Villiers St, **T** 021-4652106, www.mercuryl.co.za *Mon, Wed-Fri 2100-late. Map 2, E10, p249* Live music venue, mostly rock but also some hip-hop acts.

V & A Waterfront Amphitheatre, outdoor venue on the Waterfront, **T** 021-4087500. *All day and night. Map 3, C11, p251* With daily concerts, live performances, mainly jazz.

Theatre

Cape Town's theatre scene has rediscovered its feet following a tricky few years of freezing government funds. Political theatre, a pivotal genre during the apartheid era, is again proving popular. But while cutting-edge productions are on the up, large-scale musicals remain the most popular form of theatre – *The Phantom of the Opera* has been as huge success in 2004. Most mainstream performances are held at the Artscape Complex, but for more thought-provoking, alternative productions try the Baxter Theatre.

Artscape, DF Malan St, Foreshore, east of the train station, **T** 021-4217839, www.artscape.co.za *Matinee and evening shows.* Major complex offering opera, theatre, classical music concerts, musicals and dance performances in three theatres: Main Theatre, Arena and the Opera House.

Baxter, Main Rd, Rondebosch, **T** 021-6857880, www.baxter.co.za *Matinee and evening shows. Map 1, C4, p246* Long-term involvement in black theatre, good reputation for supporting community theatre, international productions and musicals.

Theatre on the Bay, Link St, Camps Bay, **T** 021-4833301, www.theatreonthebay.co.za *Map 4, F3, p253* Range of alternative shows with lots of cabaret, licensed, interesting mix of plays, comedy and musicals.

Celebrations are a serious business in Cape Town, and during the summer months you'll be hard pressed to find a festival-free weekend. The city makes the most of its beautiful setting, with almost all events taking place outdoors. Street carnivals and festivals compete with cultural and sporting events, although perhaps the best known event is the Karnaval in January, a street parade of competing minstrel bands. Other festivals to look out for is the young and vibey Long Street Carnival, the excellent Jazz festival held in March, and of course the famous summer concerts held at Kirstenbosch Botanical Gardens. Surprisingly, publicity is often limited and you may only hear about an event after it has taken place, but the *Cape Times* usually has good up-to-date information on what's on, or check www.capetownevents.co.za The winter months are a lot quieter, although this is the best time to visit Hermanus for its superb whale watching and its Whale Festival.

January

Karnaval (2nd), popularly known as the Coon Carnival (despite its derogatory connotations), begins in the Bo-Kaap district and ends up in the Green Point Stadium. It is without doubt the city's most popular festival. The procession of competing minstrel bands, complete with painted faces, straw boaters and bright satin suits, is quite a spectacle.

Cape to Rio yacht race starts on the first weekend of January. This mammoth annual event starts in Cape Town and attracts much of the world's sailing fraternity – accommodation gets booked up months in advance.

J&B Metropolitan Handicap, www.jbmet.co.za, held on the last Saturday of the month, is South Africa's major horse-racing meet at Kenilworth Race Course.

February

Cape Town Pride, www.capetownpride.co.za, takes place on the last weekend of the month, starting with a gay pride parade touring the city centre and culminating in a street party going on until the early hours in Green Point.

March

Cape Town Festival, www.capetownfestival.co.za, week-long arts and cultural festival held at the end of the month, various venues throughout the city.

North Sea Jazz Festival, www.nsjfcapetown.com, is held on the last weekend of the month. This is the second leg of the North Sea festival (held in the Hague) and is the city's biggest annual jazz event. Held in the Convention Centre, there are usually four stages featuring a weekend's worth of local and international jazz artists, from local legends like Hugh Masekela to international acts like Elvis Costello and Jamie Cullum.

Cape Argus Pick 'n' Pay Cycle Tour, www.cycletour.co.za, is held on a Saturday in this month and is the world's largest timed cycling event. The tour follows a gruelling circuit around Table Mountain to False Bay, across the mountains and along Chapman's Peak Drive to the Atlantic Seaboard and back into the centre of town. Much of the city is closed to motorists for the day.

Two Oceans Marathon, www.twooceansmarathon.org.za, held on the last weekend of the month, is a very popular race covering 56 km and following a similar course to the Argus Cycle Tour (hence the name Two Oceans). It is similar to the London Marathon, in that there are nearly 10,000 competitors, many of which are running for charity, so expect the usual wacky costumes. Again, much of the city is closed to motorists.

August

Cape Times Wine Festival takes place on the V & A Waterfront on the last weekend of the month. There are 300 wines to taste from 85 estates plus a cheese hall.

September

Hermanus Whale Festival, www.whalefestival.co.za, takes place during the last week of the month and marks the beginning of the calving season of Southern Right Whales. This is in essence a community festival but attracts visitors from all around the Cape. The festivities kick off with an open-air concert at the Old Harbour, and continues with theatre, comedy, live music and sporting events (including a mini-marathon) held throughout the week.

Stellenbosch Festival, **T** 021-8833891, is a three-day music and arts event concentrating on chamber music and art exhibitions.

October

Cape Times/FNB Big Walk, www.bigwalk.co.za, takes place on a weekend in the middle of the month. It is the world's largest timed walk, with an estimated 20,000 people taking part. The walk, marketed as a fun-walk but with a more serious, longer walk added on for sporty types, has been going on for some time, having started in 1903, and is aimed specifically at raising money for charities.

Smirnoff International Comedy Festival, held at the Baxter Theatre, is a three-week-long festival following a similar event in Johannesburg. There is a nightly Smirnoff show, featuring between five and 10 stand-up comedians, including local talent and British, American and Australian imports. The standard is generally very high, as is the demand for tickets, so be sure to book ahead. There are also a couple of individual stand-up shows at other venues around town.

Simon van der Stel Festival, **T** 021-8097216, held every year on the Fri and Sat nearest to 14 Oct, Simon van der Stel's birthday. Horsemen parade in traditional dress and target shooting and other activities depicting the era are acted out on the *Braak*.

Stellenbosch Wine Festival, **T** 021-8554750, takes place in the last week of the month, is an annual event to promote local award-winning wines along with traditional rural cuisine.

November

Nedbank Summer Concerts are held at the Josephine Mill, Newlands, every Sunday from November through to February. A whole range of musical performances: classical, jazz, folk, swing and choral.

December

Obz Festival, held on a Saturday at the beginning of the month, is a one-day street party held in the bohemian suburb of Observatory. The main stage is set up on Lower Main Street, and features non-stop live music from local jazz and funk bands, plus stand-up comedy and some rock music. There are also dozens of stalls selling second-hand clothes, trendy bags and jewellery, plus food and drink stands. All of the bars and cafés open their doors and hold all-night parties. The festival has a distinctly local feel, although it attracts the young and hip from all round Cape Town.

Long Street Carnival, www.longstreet.co.za, held for a weekend in the middle of the month, is another street party, held on buzzing Long Street. Several stages are set up along the road and down some of the side streets, featuring live music (mostly rock bands and techno music) and stand-up comedy. There are also a couple of fairground rides and a number of stalls selling clothes, music and food. Although the festival can be rather forlorn during the day, it really fills up in the evenings.

Mother City Queer Project Costume Party, www.mcqp.co.za, held on a Saturday night at the beginning of the month, is a vast costume party and the biggest gay event in town. Basically an all-night dance event, this is one of the best parties in Cape Town, with several stages playing techno, house, funk and 70s disco hits.

Festivals and events

Ten years?
That's a very young democracy.
If a child is ten years old,
you don't let them play in traffic.

Pieter Dirk Uys,
South Africa's most famous satirical performer,
commenting on his country.

The annual theme guarantees outrageous and hilarious costumes and an upbeat atmosphere. The venue changes every year, although regulars hope a repeat of 2004's incongruous location: the Castle of Good Hope.

Clifton Challenge, on Clifton Beach 4 on a Saturday in the middle of the month, is a fitness challenge between the Springbok rugby team and local Clifton lifesavers. This is *the* event for the beautiful people, attracting the usual well-heeled beach crowd, and entails a day of tug-of-war and similar 'tests', plus live music and competitions. There is also the 'Mr and Mrs Clifton' competition, a rather archaic beauty show with inevitable bronzed blonds winning the cherished titles.

Kirstenbosch Summer Concerts, www.nbi.ac.za, take place every Sunday from December until March. These are undoubtedly a summer highlight and should not be missed. The outdoor concerts are held on rolling lawns in Kirstenbosch Botanical Gardens, with the unrivalled backdrop of the mountains and gardens. The atmosphere is typically relaxed: visitors spread blankets on the grass and enjoy boozy picnics while listening to the music. The concerts ranges from popular classics and opera to jazz, world music and South African favourites such as Johnny Clegg.

Cape Town represents good value for money for shoppers, and many well-heeled visitors come here for little else. The *Cape Times* and *Argus* newspapers run regular gleeful stories reporting on individual tourists who spend millions of Rand in a few days' visit. While this is rather above most visitors' budgets, stocking up on curios, clothes and crafts is well worth it. The main shopping area is the V & A Waterfront, which is crammed with clothes, souvenir, music and crafts shops – but prices are above the average here. The city centre also has a good range, with a couple of craft markets, some excellent second-hand book, antique and bric-a-brac shops and a handful of trendy clothes shops. Capetonians stick to their trusted shopping malls: the largest and glitziest is Century City off the N1 to Belville, 15 minutes from the city centre, home also to Ratanga Junction, see Kids, p214. More accessible and not quite as overwhelming is Cavendish Square in Claremont. Most of the better clothes chains and boutiques are in Cape Town's shopping malls. Long St and Kloof St are good bets for alternative clothes and accessories.

Arts, crafts and curios

African Image, 52 Burg St, **T** 021-4238385. *0900-1800 weekdays, 0830-1600 Sat, closed Sun. Map 2, A8, p249* Not your everyday curio shop, with tribal art and crafts which could well be an investment, plus quirky souvenirs like coke-bottle-top bags and chickens made from colourful plastic bags.

Greenmarket Square Market *0800-1700 Mon-Fri, 0900-1400 Sat Map 2, A8, p249* Lively market in the centre of town selling crafts, textiles and clothes from across the continent.

Heartworks, 98 Kloof St, **T** 021-4248419. *0900-1700 weekdays, 0830-1300 Sat, closed Sun. Map 2, E3, p248* Hand-made crafts, mainly from Kwazulu-Natal, including interesting woven baskets, bangles and bags.

Monkeybiz, The Pinnacle, corner of Burg and Castle streets, **T** 021-4260145, www.monkeybiz.co.za. *0800-1900 Mon-Fri, 0830-1400 Sat, 0900-1300 Sun. Map 2, A8, p249* Something of a local sensation, Monekybiz creates employment for township women (many of them HIV Positive), who create beautiful and quirky one-off bead works, including figures, animals and accessories. Sold at the Tourist Office.

Out of this World, V &A Waterfront, **T** 021-4213507. *0900-2100. Map 3, B11, p251* One of many African arts and crafts shops at the Waterfront, but with a better value and more tasteful selection than most. Can arrange for overseas shipping.

Peter Visser Gallery , cnr Long and Church Sts, **T** 021-4237870. *Map 2, A7, p249* Celebrated local gallery selling antiques and expensive contemporary African art and ceramics.

Red Shed, part of Victoria Wharf shopping centre. *0830-1800 Mon-Sat, 0830-1600 Sun. Map 3, B11, p251* Handful of local craftsmen selling painted ostrich eggs, decorated animals hides and the like. Popular, but goods are of suspect taste.

The Pan African Market, Long St, **T** 021-4242957. *Map 2, A8, p249* Centre selling crafts from around Africa and good local crafts made from recycled material, beadwork, ceramics. Café specializing in African food.

Streetwires, 77 Shortmarket St, T021-4262475, www.streetwires.co.za *0830-1700 Mon-Fri. Map 3, H9, p251* Building housing a wire sculpture co-operative, useful place to browse these interesting South Africa craft works without feeling under pressure from the usual street vendors.

Books and maps

Bell-Roberts, 199 Loop St, **T** 021-4221100. *0830-1700 weekdays, 0830-1400 Sat, closed Sun. Map 2, A7, p249* Gallery, café and publishing house specializing in art books.

Clarke's Books, 211 Long St, **T** 021-4235739, www.clarkesbooks.co.za. *0830-1700 weekdays, 0830-1400 Sat, closed Sun. Map 2, B7, p249* A mass of antiquarian, second-hand and new books. A must for any book lover.

CNA (Central News Agencies), city-wide chain. Carry a reasonable stock of guide books, glossy coffee table publications, some colourful maps, foreign newspapers and magazines.

Exclusive Books, city-wide chain. Upmarket, with branches in most shopping centres selling a wide choice of paperbacks and coffee table books. Good on South African history and culture.

Drink in the scenery
The Winelands, surrounding Cape Town, are a beautiful region of historic vineyards and quiet farms, nestling in fertile valleys.

Roll out the barrels
Sample world-class wines in the Cape's scenic Winelands.

Bowled over
Sit back and gaze at the marvellous view of the City Bowl from the summit of Table Mountain.

Sea and be seen
The bronzed and beautiful flock to Clifton's four white-sand beaches.

Sundowner
Enjoy a drink at La Med, Clifton's best-known bar, as the sun sets over the Cape.

Beach life
The Cape's Atlantic coast is lined with a series of glorious white-sand beaches, lapped by startlingly blue (and eye-wateringly cold) waters.

The Map Studio, Struik House, 80 McKenzie Rd, Gardens, **T** 021-4624360, www.mapstudio.co.za. *0830-1700 weekdays, 0830-1300 Sat, closed Sun.* Map 2, E9, p249 Tourist maps of towns and regions as well as official survey maps.

Traveller's Bookshop, Alfred Mall, Victoria Wharf, **T** 021-4256880. *0830-1900 Mon-Sat, 0900-1630 Sun.* Map 3, C10, p251 Excellent selection of travel literature, guidebooks and maps.

Clothes

The larger shopping malls have some international clothing stores, such as *Guess*, *Diesel* and *Benetton*, usually stocking the same clothes as at home, but at slightly cheaper prices. More mainstream shops such as *Gap* or *H&M* have not made it to South Africa yet. *Woolworths* is the South African equivalent of *Marks and Spencers* and stocks similar clothes and food at lower prices.

Cavendish Square, Claremont, **T** 021-6743050. *0800-2100.* Map 1, C4, p246 Slightly more upmarket mall with clothes, household and book stores. Popular with trendy teenagers and well-coifed Claremont ladies.

India Jane, Station Rd, Kalk Bay **T** 021-6837607. *0830-1700 weekdays, 0830-1300 Sat, closed Sun.* Map 1, G3, p247 One of a small Cape Town boutique chain selling expensive designer items, lots of one-off pieces.

Labels for Less , 10 Cavendish St, **T** 021-6831162. *0830-1700 weekdays, 0830-1500 Sat, closed Sun.* Map 1, C4, p246 Designer clothes at sale prices year-round.

Mememe , 279 Long St, **T** 021-4240001. *0900-1700 weekdays, 0900-1500 Sat, closed Sun* Map 2, B6, p249 Tiny designer-owned boutique selling über-cool dresses, skirts and accessories by local South African designers.

Misfit , 192 Long St, **T** 021-4225646. *0900-1700 weekdays, 0900-1500 Sat, closed Sun Map 2, B6, p249* The latest designs for well-heeled twenty-somethings, plus trendy shoes and sandals.

Scar, 22 Kloof St, T021-4225085 *0900-1700 weekdays, 0900-1600 Sat, closed Sun. Map 2, D5, p248* One of the best known of this area's quirky shops and still the place to head for eccentric one-off designs, 1980s-inspired skirts and tops, groovy bikinis, bags and perspex jewellery.

Victoria Wharf, Victoria and Alfred Waterfront, **T** 021-4087600, www.waterfront.co.za. *Map 3, B11, p251* Cape Town's best known shopping mall, always busy with tourists and well-heeled locals. Units of designer and high-street clothes selling their wares marginally cheaper than can be bought back home.

Jewellery

South Africa's biggest export is gold, and the world's most famous diamond company, De Beers, is based here. Jewellery is thus quite a big draw for shoppers, although designs are usually quite traditional and pieces are not as good value as one might expect. Ethnic jewellery is widely available and very popular with visitors. **Greenmarket Square Market** (see p195) has a good range of African jewellery, such as glass-bead necklaces and pieces made of ostrich shell, as well as imported Asian jewellery and silver rings and necklaces sold by local designers.

Jewel Africa, 170 Buitengracht St, Bo-Kaap, **T** 021-4245141, www.jewelafrica.com, *0830-1700 Mon-Fri, 0900-1300 Sat. Map 2, A6, p249* Africa's largest jewellery showroom with a wide range of good quality gold, silver, platinum and precious stones. Specializes in personal designs which can be completed in 24 hours, also features Kraal Kraft – African crafts and souvenirs.

The Pan African Market, Long St, **T** 021-4242957. *0830-1700 Mon-Sat. Map 2, A8, p249* Arts and crafts centre, also has a range of good value jewellery from across the continent, including beadwork and Masai necklaces.

Philip Zetler, 54 St George's Mall, **T** 021-4322771. *0900-1700 Mon-Fri, 0900-1300 Sat. Map 2, A8, p249* Husband and wife team selling diamonds, jewellery pieces, antique jewellery and watches.

Uwe Koetter, 4th Floor, Amway House, Dock Road, **T** 021-4257770, www.uwekoetter.co.za. *0830-1700 Mon-Fri, 0900-1300 Sat. Map 3, C10, p251* Traditional high-quality jewellery design, specializing in exclusive pieces – no piece is made twice. Emphasis is on diamonds, but also has some less expensive pieces. Workshop tours available.

Markets

Church Street Market, between Long and Burg sts. *0900-1400, Mon-Sat. Map 2, A7, p249* Offbeat antiques. Most interesting pieces shown on Fridays and Saturdays.

Grand Parade Market *0800-1400, Wed and Sat. Map 2, B9, p249* A general market selling clothes, fabrics and flowers, which takes over the large parade ground in front of the old City Hall.

Greenmarket Square Market *0800-1700 Mon-Fri, 0900-1400 Sat. Map 2, A8, p249* A lively flea market on a picturesque cobbled square, formerly a fruit and vegetable market, flanked by several terrace cafés.

Green Point Market, beside Green Point stadium. *0800-1700 Sun only. Map 3, C7, p251* Good for curios, bags and textiles. Buskers entertain the crowds.

Waterfront Explorers Market, V & A Waterfront. *0830-1800 Mon-Sat, 0830-1600 Sun. Map 3, D10, p251* Arts and crafts.

Music

The African Music Store, 90a Long St, **T** 021-4260857, africanmusic@sybaweb.co.za. *Mon-Fri 0900-1800, Sat 1000-1600. Map 2, A7, p249* The place to head to for African music. Stocks an excellent choice by major Southern African artists as well as compilations and reggae. The helpful staff are are happy to let you listen to any number of CDs before purchasing. Recommended.

Wine

Individual estates are the best places to buy wine, see pp85-94. Most offer shipping abroad as part of their service. Transport and taxes can be pricey (expect to pay from R1,500 for the transport of 12 bottles to Europe), although the good value for money of the actual wines makes it quite tempting. Larger supermarkets and 'bottle shops' also stock most good South African wines.

Vaughan Johnson's Wine Shop, V & A Waterfront, **T** 021-4192121. *0830-1900 Mon-Sat, 1000-1700 Sun. Map 3, C10, p251* Has an excellent selection and a reliable shipping service.

Waterfront World of Wine, Clocktower Center, V & A Waterfront, **T** 021-418001. *0830-1900 Mon-Sat, 1000-1700 Sun. Map 3, C10, p251* Comprehensive wine selection, plus offers tastings of up to twenty wines.

Cape Town has a serious outdoors, get-fit lifestyle – the entire population seems to spend its free time jogging along the beaches, strapping itself on to bungee ropes or hiking up Table Mountain. Its equiclimate and excellent facilities make it a great destination for adventure sports – cage diving with great white sharks, sandboarding on huge dunes, kitesurfing with the notorious southeasterly wind and paragliding from the top of Lion's Head – as well as more sedate pursuits such as watching a cricket match or playing a round of golf. There are also a number of marathons and cycle races held during summer, although the most popular sport with young Capetonians remains surfing. Most of the backpacker hostels promote an impressive choice of activities. One of the best places to visit and find out about all the options on offer is a store called **Adventure Village**, 229 Long St, **T** 021-4241580, www.adventure-village.co.za

Abseiling

Abseil Africa, Table Mountain, **T** 021-4241580, part of Adventure Village. *0900-1700. Map 1, C3, p246* Operates the world's highest and longest commercial abseil – 112 m down Table Mountain.

Bungee jumping

Although it's no longer possible to bungee jump from the Table Mountain cable car, South Africa does boast the world's highest commercial jump about a day's drive from Cape Town. The **Bloukrans Bungee Jump** is on the Garden Route to the west of Tsitsikamma National Park. The jump is an impressive 216 metres and costs R550. Contact the operators, Face Adrenaline, **T** 021-2811458, www.faceadrenalin.com, or the Adventure Village (see opposite).

Cricket

Newlands, **T** 021-6836420, www.wpca.cricket.org *Map 1, C4, p246* Despite considerable redevelopment, Cape Town's famous test match ground still has a few of its famous old oak trees, and it is still possible to watch a game from a grassy bank with Table Mountain as a backdrop.

Fishing

Deep-sea fishing is big business around the Cape. The most common catches are mako shark, long fin tuna and yellowtail, but there are strict rules governing all types of fishing. The simplest way of dealing with permits and regulations is by booking through a charter company.

Sports

Big Game Fishing Safaris, 9 Daisy Way, Newlands, **T** 021-6742203, skipper@gamefish.co.za *Map 1, C4, p246*
Daily excursions on a 12-m catamaran including crayfish lunch. Specializes in tuna and swordfish fishing.

Nauticat Charters, Hout Bay Harbour, **T** 021-7907278, www.nauticatcharters.co.za *Map 1, E1, p246* Game fishing and boat charters.

Hooked on Africa , Hout Bay Harbour, **T** 021-7905332, www.hookedonafrica.co.za *Map 1, E1, p246* Deep-sea tuna trips and crayfish charters. Can also organize fly-fishing trips in the Winelands.

Golf

Expect to pay green fees of around R200 for 18 holes. The following is a selection of the golf clubs which are open to overseas visitors. For further details contact the **Western Province Golf Union**, **T** 021-6861668, wpga@global.co.za.

Milnerton Golf Club, Bridge Rd, Milnerton, **T** 021-5521047. Length: 6,011 m, par 72. Green fees about R200. This is a true links course in the shadow of Table Mountain; watch your par when the wind blows.

Mowbray Golf Club, Ratenberg Rd, Mowbray, **T** 021-6853018, www.mowbraygolfclub.co.za *Map 1, C4, p246* One of the oldest clubs, hosts national championships, a par 74 course with plenty of trees, bunkers and water holes.

Rondebosch Golf Club, Klipfontein, Rondebosch, **T** 021-6894176, rgc@mweb.co.za *Map 1, C4, p246* A tidy course with the Black River flowing through it.

Royal Cape Golf Club, 174 Ottery Rd, Wynberg, **T** 021-7616551. *Map 1, D4, p246* Length: 6,174 m, par 74. Expect to pay about R250 for green fees. An old course which has been the venue for major professional tournaments.

Simon's Town Country Club, **T** 021-7861233. *Map 1, I3, p247* A nine-hole, 18-tee course, a real test for anyone not used to playing in very windy conditions.

Hiking

Active Africa , **T** 021-7888750, www.active-africa.com Leading operator organizing walking tours on Table Mountain and Cape Point, plus hiking trips to the Winelands and the Garden Route. Also has guided climbs on Table Mountain; all transport, food and guides included in price.

Due South, **T** 083-2584824 (mob), www.hikesandtours.co.za, ask for John or Cathy. Organize half- and full-day walking trips up Table Mountain. Rates include transport to/from the start point for your hike, snacks and water, and a packed lunch on full-day hikes.

Table Mountain Safaris, **T** 082-3397047 (mob), www.tablemountainsafaris.co.za Hikes and day walks on the mountain, in Newlands Forest and up Chapman's Peak.

Horse riding

There are plenty of interesting riding trails around the city, and Noordhoek Beach is especially popular at sundown. These operators organize short rides or day trips along Noordhoek and further afield.

Nordhoek Beach Horse Rides, **T** 082-7741191 (mob), www.horseriding.co.za *Map 1, F2, p246*

Sleepy Hollow Horse Riding, **T** 021-7892341.

Kitesurfing

The Cape's strong winds have made it a very popular site for kitesurfing. The best spot is Dolphin Beach at Table View, just to the north of the city, where winds are strong and the waves are perfect for jumping.

Cape Sports Centre, Langebaan Lagoon, **T** 022-7721114, www.capesport.co.za Extreme watersports centre, offering tuition and equipment.

Windsports, Tableview, **T** 021-5562765, www.windsports.co.za Equipment rental and tuition, starting at R350 for an hour.

Kloofing

Kloofing (canyoning) involves hiking, boulder-hopping and swimming along mountain rivers. It is very popular on and around Table Mountain.

Day Trippers, 8 Pineway, Pinelands, **T** 021-5114766, www.daytrippers.co.za Active tours popular with backpackers, kloofing can be arranged as part of a trip.

Mountain biking

Downhill Adventures, **T** 021-4220388, www.downhill adventures.co.za Organizes a range of mountain biking excursions, including the popular Table Mountain double descent (90% downhill), rides around Cape Point and the Winelands Meander. Also have bike rentals.

Mountain climbing

Mountain Club of South Africa, 97 Hatfield St (close to the Jewish museum), **T** 021-4653412, www.cap.mcsa.org.za *Map 2, D7, p249* Good source of information on climbing in Cape Town and throughout South Africa.

Active Africa,**T** 021-7888750, www.active-africa.com   Organizes climbs on Table Mountain.

Paragliding

Paragliding from Lions Head is very popular, with gliders landing by the sea between Clifton and Camps Bay. For tandem paragliding sessions contact **Para-Pax**, **T** 021-4617070, www.parapax.com

Rugby

Western Province Rugby Football Union ground, Boundary Rd, Newlands, **T** 021-6894921. *Map 1, C4, p246*. International games are played here. Tickets for major games can be bought through **Computicket**, **T** 0839158000, www.computicket.co.za

Sailing

Regattas are regularly held in Table Bay. The following clubs are for members only, but they do accommodate visitors if they are members of an affiliated international club.

Royal Cape Yacht Club, **T** 021-4211354. Organizes regattas and holds talks and social events.

False Bay Yacht Club, **T** 021-7861703, www.fbyc.co.za Based in Simon's Town, offers sailing and fishing trips.

Hout Bay Yacht Club, **T** 021-7903110, www.hbyc.co.za Weekly social sailing, plus training courses.

Sandboarding

Try the latest addition to board sports on sand dunes. It is not very fast and can be frustrating if you're used to snow, but it can be fun.

Downhill Adventures, **T** 021-4220388, www.downhill adventures.co.za Organizes day trips to dunes about an hour from Cape Town.

Scuba diving

The Cape waters are cold but are often very clear and good for wreck and reef diving. A number of dive companies also specialize in great white shark cage dives along the coast.

Dusky Dive Academy, 33 Castle St, **T** 021-4261622. *Map 3, H9, p251* Instruction for beginners.

Scuba Shack, 289 Long St, **T/F** 021-4249368, www.scuba-shack.co.za *Map 2, B6, p248* Full range of PADI-recognized instruction and equipment hire, as well as organized tours to the best dive sites and great white shark cage dives. Also has an office on False Bay (**T** 021-7827358).

Table Bay Diving, V & A Waterfront, **T** 021-4191780, boatrips@iafrica.com   *Map 3, B11, p251*   Dive charters and full range of PADI courses, and sells scuba and snorkelling gear.

Skydiving

Skydive Cape Town , **T** 092-8006290 (mob), www.skydivecapetown.za.net Offers tandem jumps and static-line courses on the West Coast.

Surfing

Surfing is a serious business in Cape Town, and there are excellent breaks catering for learners right through to experienced surf rats. Some of the best breaks are on Long Beach, Kommetjie, Noordhoek, Llandudno, Kalk Bay, Muizenberg and Bloubergstrand. Daily surf report: **T** 021-7881350.

Downhill Adventures, **T** 021-4220388, www.downhill adventures.co.za Organize day and multi-day courses as well as 'Secret Surf Spots' tours.

Adventure Village, **T** 021-4241580, www.adventure-village .co.za Offer good surfing advice.

Real Cape Adventures, **T** 082-8684889, surfup@mweb.co.za Surf lessons and guided surfing trips to the best spots in the area.

Swimming

The beaches on the Atlantic Seaboard are almost always too cold to swim in – even during the hottest months, the water temperatures rarely creep above 14°C. False Bay, however, is always a good 5°C warmer, and is perfectly pleasant for a dip during summer. Additionally, a number of beaches have artificial rock pools built by the water, which, although rather murky, can be perfect for paddling children. There are some very good municipal swimming pools in Cape Town, in Newlands, Sea Point and Woodstock. All are open air and have views of the mountain.

Tennis

Green Point Lawn Tennis Club, Green Point Common, **T** 021-4349527. *Map 3, B8, p251* Casual popular courts.

River Club Centre, Liesbeek Parkway, Observatory, **T** 021-4486117. *Map 7, A6, p255* Friendly club, no equipment hire, book in advance.

The Western Province Tennis Association, **T** 021-6863055. Can provide details of clubs and competitions.

Windsurfing

Langebaan has the best reputation for surfable winds on the Cape; the southeasterly roars between September and April making this the windsurfing season. In March there is a Boardsailing Marathon in False Bay, while Big Bay at Blouberg is a good spot for wave-jumping. Daily windsurf report: **T** 082-2346324 (mob).

Windsports, Tableview, **T** 082-5562765, www.windsports.co.za Equipment rental and tuition.

Cape Sports Centre, Langebaan Lagoon, **T** 022-7721114, www.capesport.co.za Extreme watersports centre based about an hour's drive north of Cape Town.

Cape Town is rated, along with Sydney and San Francisco, as one of the 'Gay Capitals' of the world. Certainly, it is the most gay- and lesbian-friendly city in Africa, with a lively scene that draws visitors from across the country and continent. There is a good range of bars, clubs and events aimed specifically at a gay crowd, many of which are the coolest in town – nights are correspondingly very popular and more mixed than you might expect.

The area around Green Point, known as De Waterkant Village, is Cape Town's gay and lesbian hotspot, and all the main bars and clubs are found along Somerset and Main roads. The main gay event and one of the best parties of the year is the **Mother City Queer Project**, www.mcqp.co.za, a fantastically extravagant costume party and rave – not to be missed if you're in town in December, especially if it's being held at the frankly bizarre venue of the Castle of Good Hope. There is also the **Cape Town Pride Festival**, www.capetownpride.co.za, in late February, with a parade touring the city centre and a street party going on until the early hours in Green Point.

March sees the successful annual nationwide gay film festival, known as **Out in Africa**, www.oia.co.za, with screenings of top gay-themed or directed films from around the world. Films are shown in Cape Town during the last two weeks of February.

An excellent guide to the gay scene is the free *Pink Map*, available at tourist offices and a number of trendy shops and bars around town. It has useful listings and up-to-date details of everything from bars and clubs to accommodation and steam baths. The tourist office also has copies of the *Cape Gay Guide*, an annual booklet with info on nightlife and accommodation. *detail* is a free monthly gay lifestyle paper distributed in gay-friendly bars, clubs and shops.

Bars and clubs

A Touch of Madness, Pepper Tree Sq, Nuttal Rd, Observatory. *1500-late. Map 7, B4, p255* Flamboyant bar and restaurant run by eccentric gay couple, lavish, ironic decor, good food, great atmosphere. A pleasant alternative to the scene at Green Point.

Confession, 27 Somerset Rd, Green Point, **T** 021-4214798, *Wed-Sun 2200-0400. Map 3, F10, p251* Swanky new club with a strange churchy theme, deep house and funk, noisy crowd.

Bar Code, 16 Hudson St, **T** 021-4215305, www.leatherbar.co.za *Daily 2200-0200. Map 3, G10, p252* Cape Town's only men's leather, uniform and jeans bar. Industrial interior, video, dark room, garden, serious cruising place.

Bronx, corner of Somerset Rd and Napier St, Green Point, www.bronx.co.za *Daily 2000-late. Map 3, F10, p251* Probably Cape Town's best-known and most popular gay bar and club, gets packed out at weekends, mostly men but women welcome, live

DJs spin out thumping techno every night, karaoke on Mon. The Pride festival usually ends here.

Buena Vista Social Café, Main Rd, Green Point, **T** 021-4330611. *Daily 1200-late. Map 3, D8, p251* Ultra-trendy Cuban-themed bar and restaurant catering to a mixed, well-heeled crowd. Great Latin music, live bands at weekend, relaxed atmosphere, good but pricey cocktails. Small entrance fee after 2200.

Café Manhattan, 74 Waterkant St, Green Point, **T** 021-4216666, www.manhattan.co.za *Daily 1100-late. Map 3, F9, p251* Vibey café and restaurant serving New York-themed snacks and meals, friendly owner Russel creates a welcoming vibe.

Chilli n' Lime, 23 Somerset Rd, Green Point, **T** 082-9734673 (mob). *Wed, Fri, Sat 2000-0400 Map 3, F10, p251* Trendy bar and club spread over two floors, young and pretentious crowd, wild goth and S&M themed nights held on Wednesdays.

Evita se Perron, Darling Station, Darling, 55 mins from Cape Town, **T** 022-4922831, www.evita.co.za *From R10*. Evita is a South African gay institution, a sort of Afrikaans Dame Edna, hosting lively events at her café-theatre, which includes Bambi's Berlin Bar, a shop, restaurant and gallery.

Jo'burg, 218 Long St, **T** 021-4220142. *Daily 1500-0300. Map 2, B6, p248* Popular bar serving pints and cocktails to a mixed crowd, gay-friendly, pool table, dance room, gets very busy at weekends, funky house and drum 'n' bass.

On Broadway, 21 Somerset Rd, Green Point, **T** 021-4188338, www.onbroadway.co.za *2000-late. Map 3, F10, p251* Cabaret and live music venue, popular for big-name drag shows like Mince (Tues and Sun evenings). Meals served.

Purgatory, Dixon St, Green Point, **T** 021-4217464. *Wed, Fri & Sat 2200-0400*. *Map 3, F10, p251* Trumpeted as a 'model's' club, this gay-friendly club attracts a mixed, stylish crowd. House music, leather sofas, cocktails – and models get in free.

Sliver, 27 Somerset Rd, Green Point, **T** 021-4215798. *Map 3, F10, p251* Trendy lounge bar, mostly gay clientele but also very popular with a trendy, mixed crowd. Relaxed atmosphere, heats up later at night. Connected to the much more raucous *Confession*, in same complex.

Tour operators

Friends of Dorothy Tours, **T** 021-4651871, www.friendsofdorothytours.co.za Gay tour company organizing day trips to Cape Point, the Winelands, whale watching tours, private or small groups.

Go Pink in Africa, **T** 021-4627771, www.gopinkinafrica.com Gay tours and accommodation throughout southern Africa.

Wanderwomen, **T** 021-6839215, www.wanderwomen.co.za Women-only tours by and for lesbians, around Cape Town and longer tours up Garden Route available.

Resources

GALACTTIC, **T** 021-4246445, www.galacttic.co.za Association of gay-related businesses promoting gay commerce.

Out in Africa, **T** 021-4659289, www.oia.co.za Annual gay film festival held in Feb-March.

q on line, www.q.co.za   South Africa's main gay and lesbian website with email access, chat rooms and a dating service.

Triangle Project, **T** 021-4483812/3. HIV testing, counselling and a library.

Cape Town's outdoor-orientated character makes it a great place to take kids, with plenty of sights that interest adults while keeping children busy. An added bonus is that many attractions offer free entrance or substantial reductions to children (usually under 16).

Cape Town's beaches have the added attraction of wildlife and activities, like penguins or surfing. Some of the best to head for are on False Bay as it has warmer and calmer waters than on the Atlantic seaboard side. Boulders Beach is safe for swimming and has the bonus of a large penguin population. Fish Hoek has a pleasant beach with small waves and a playground. On the Atlantic side, Camps Bay has a tidal pool and shady, grassy areas. Noordhoek is too rough for swimming, but is a great place for kite-flying or a horse ride. As well as outdoor activities, a number of the museums cater for children, with interactive displays and child-friendly exhibits. There are also the high-octane attractions of Ratanga Junction, complete with hair-raising roller coasters as well as gentler rides for toddlers.

Sights, activities and excursions

Table Mountain Aerial Cableway, **T** 012-4248181, www.tablemountain.net *0830-2000/2200 (last car down at 1900 in winter), R110 for an adult return.* R55 for children under 18. *Map 1, C3, p246 See also p31* The dizzying trip to the top is one of Cape Town's highlights and guaranteed to excite children.

South Africa Museum and Planetarium, Company's Garden, **T** 021-4243330. *1000-1700. R8, under 16s free. Planetarium shows Mon-Fri 1400, Sat and Sun, 1300, 1430, late showing on Tue 2000, R20, children R6. Map 2, C6, p248 See also p34* Although the ethnography and archaeology sections may test kids' patience, the major exhibits feature extensive examples of Southern African wildlife as well as dinosaur fossils and a huge whale room, with several full-size skeletons and a whale-song well. A soon-to-open addition to the natural history section is 'Shark World', an interactive multi-media area exploring the world of sharks.

Two Oceans Aquarium, Dock Rd, **T** 021-4183823, www.aquarium.co.za *0930-1800. Daily feeds at 1530. R55, under 17s R25. Map 3, C9, p251 See also p50* This is highly recommended and very popular for families. The displays are fascinating and simply labelled. The basement holds the Alpha Activity Centre, where free puppet shows and face painting keep children busy. There are also touch pools, where children can pick up spiky starfish and slimy sea slugs. The highlight is the predators exhibit, holding ragged-tooth sharks, eagle rays and some impressively large hunting fish.

Ratanga Junction, Century City, **T** 0861-200300, www.ratanga.co.za. *Wed-Fri and Sun 1000-1700, Sat 1000-1800 (extended during school holidays). Follow the N1 to Belville and take exit 10 for Century City. R90, children R45.* South Africa's largest theme park is a recreation of a 19th-century mining town, crammed with impressive thrill rides, roller coasters and family rides. Tickets allow as many rides as you want. Some have a height restriction.

MTN Science Centre, Century City, **T** 021-5298100, www.mtnsciencentre.org.za *0930-1800, until 2000 on Fri and Sat. Follow the N1 to Belville and take exit 10 for Century City. R24, children R20.* This is South Africa's first (and only) interactive science centre, aimed at children to help them learn about scientific discoveries and technological innovations. There are over 280 displays, most of them interactive, as well as an auditorium, a camera obscura and an exhibition hall.

Boulders Beach, **T** 021-7862329, boulders@parks-sa.co.za *0800-1700. R15, free at other times. Map 1, I3, p247 See also p73* Boulders is one of the most attractive beaches on False Bay and also the best place for spotting African penguins on the Peninsula. Hundreds of birds live on the beach, taking little notice of their sunbathing neighbours. Excellent swimming beach with no waves.

Kirstenbosch Botanical Gardens, **T** 021-7998783, weekends **T** 021-7998800, www.nbi.ac.za *Sep-Mar 0800-1900, Apr-Aug 0800-1800. R20, children R8. Map 1, D3, p246 See also p63* South Africa's oldest, largest and most exquisite botanical garden is the perfect spot for a family picnic. The rolling lawns and shady areas are great for toddlers to run about on, while the Fragrance garden or the Medicinal Plants garden will interest older kids. There are also plenty of hidden forest trails, perfect for playing hide and seek.

Cape of Good Hope , **T** 021-7018692, www.cpnp.co.za *0600-1800 Oct-Mar, 0700-1700 Apr-Sep. R35. Map 1, K3, p247 See also p58* The nature reserve is a wonderful area to spend a day wandering and picnicking. There are some easy walks and a number of deserted beaches perfect for flying a kite.

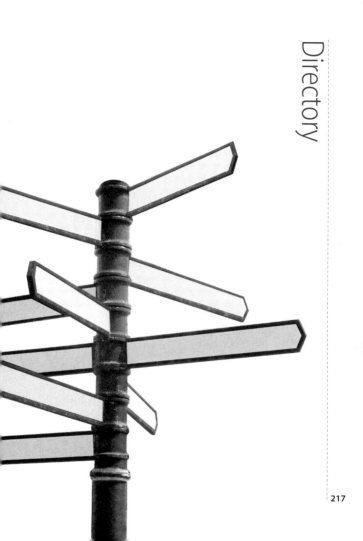

Airline offices

Air Namibia, **T** 021-9362755, www.airnamibia.com. **Air Zimbabwe**, **T** 011-6157017, www.airzim.co.zw. **British Airways**, **T** 021-9369000, www.britishairways.com. **Comair**, **T** 011-9210222, www.ba.co.za. **Egypt Air**, **T** 021-4618056, www.egyptair.com. **KLM**, **T** 021-4211870, www.klm.com. **Kulula**, **T** 0861-585852, www.kulula.com. **Lufthansa**, **T** 9348534, www.lufthansa.com. **Malaysia Airlines**, **T** 021-4198010, www.malaysiaairlines.com. **Singapore Airlines**, **T** 021-6740601, www.singaporeair.com. **South African Airways**, **T** 021-11-9785313, www.flysaa.com. **Swissair**, **T** 0860-040506, www.swiss.com. **Virgin Atlantic**, **T** 011-3403500, www.virgin-atlantic.com.

Banks and ATMs

Only change money in hotels as a last resort as their exchange rates are unbelievably poor. There are plenty of 24-hour cash machines (ATMs) throughout the city, making it easy to keep in funds. There are also a number of banks where you can cash traveller's cheques. All the main branches are open weekdays 0830-1530 and Sat 0800-1100. The following are the principal branches in Cape Town city centre (Adderley Street). **ABSA**, **First National Bank**, **Standard Bank**. There are two main bureaux de change in Cape Town. **Amex**, **T** 021-4193917, Alfred Mall, V & A Waterfront, will receive and hold mail for card holders, open Mon to Sat 0900-1700. The other main bureaux is **Rennies Travel** (Thomas Cook representatives), 2 St George's Mall, **T** 021-4181206, open Mon-Fri 0830-1700, Sat 0900-1200. They also have a branch at the Waterfront, on the upper level of Victoria Wharf, **T** 021-4183744. Rennies Travel also provides all the usual services of a travel agent.

Bicycle hire

See Sports, p202.

Car hire

Adelphi Car Rental, 94 Main Rd, Sea Point, T 021-4396144, adelphi@intekom.co.za **Atlantic Car Hire**, T 021-9344600, www.atlanticcarhire.co.za **Avis**, T 0861021111.
Budget, 63 Strand St, **T** 0861016622, www.budget.co
Cape Car Hire, 217 Lansdowne Rd, Claremont, **T** 021-6832441, www.capecarhire.co.za **Europcar**, 33 Heerengracht, Foreshore, **T** 021-4180670, www.europcar.com **The Happy Beetle Company**, T 021-4264170, www.thehappybeetleco.com, original VW Beetles. **Hertz**, T 021-4009650, www.hertz.com **Imperial**, Strand St, **T** 021-4215190. **Tempest**, **T** 086113100.

Credit card lines

Stolen credit cards: **T** 0800-990418 (Mastercard), **T** 0800-990475 (Visa), **T** 0869-003768 (Amex).

Cultural institutions

British Council, T 021-4606660, www.britishcouncil.org /southafrica **Iziko Museums of Cape Town**, www.museums.org.za/iziko **University of Cape Town**, www.uct.ac.za **South Africa Cultural Heritage**, www.saculturalheritage.org **South African Public Library**, T 021-4246320, www.ulsa.ac.za

Dentists

Hope Street Dental Clinic, T 021-4654017. **Med Pages**, list of health care practitioners, T 021-4181474, www.medpages.co.za

Electricity

Runs on 220/230V, 50hz AC. Sockets are unique round-pinned three-pronged plugs. Plug converters can be bought in electric goods shops and Clicks chemists. Most hotel rooms have 110 volt outlets for electric shavers.

Embassies

Most foreign representatives have their head offices in either Pretoria or Johannesburg, but many countries also have representatives in Cape Town.

Australia, 14th Floor, BP Centre, Thibault Square, **T** 021-4195425. **Belgium**, Vogue House, Thibault Square, **T** 021-4194690. **Canada**, Reserve Bank Building, 30 Hout St, **T** 021-4235240. **Denmark**, Southern Life Centre, Riebeeck St, **T** 021-4196936. **Finland**, Lincoln Rd, Oranjezicht, **T** 021-4614732. **France**, 2 Dean St Gardens, **T** 021-4231575. **Germany**, 825 St Martini Gardens, Queen Victoria St, **T** 021-4242410. **India**, The Terraces, 34 Bree St, **T** 021-4198110. **Italy**, 2 Greys Pass, Gardens, **T** 021-4241256. **Japan**, Main Tower, Standard Bank Centre, Heerenracht, T 021-4251695. **Mozambique**, 45 Castle St, **T** 021-4262944, visas issued within 24 hrs. **Netherlands**, 100 Strand St, **T** 021-4215660. **Portugal**, Standard Bank Centre, Herzog Blvd, **T** 021-4180080. **Russian Federation**, Southern Life Centre, Hertzog Blvd, **T** 021-4183656. **Spain**, 37 Short Market St, **T** 021-4222415. **Sweden**, 10th Floor, Southern Life Centre, 8 Riebeeck St, **T** 021-4181276. **Switzerland**, **T** 021-4261040. **UK**, Southern Life Centre, 8 Riebeeck St, **T** 021-4052400. **USA**, 4th Floor, Broadway Ind Centre, Heerengracht, **T** 021-4214280. **Zimbabwe**, 55c Kuyper St, **T** 021-4614710.

Emergency numbers

Police: **T** 10111. **Tourist Assistance Police Unit**: **T** 021-4215116 (not 24 hours). **Ambulance**: **T** 10177. **Mountain rescue**: **T** 021-9489900. **Sea rescue**: **T** 021-4053500. **National AIDS Helpline**: **T** 0800-012322 (24 hours).

Hospitals

Casualty facilities available at: **Groote Schuur**, Observatory, **T** 021-4049111, 24 hrs; **Somerset**, Green Point, **T** 021-4026911; **Tygerberg**, Bellville, **T** 021-9384911; **Red Cross Children's Hospital**, Mowbray, **T** 021-6895277.

Internet/email

Internet access is available at backpacker hostels, **Postnet** branches (see below) and at the main tourist office. **Virtual Turtle** is a popular internet café on the first floor of the Purple Turtle building, Short Market St, **T** 021-4241037. **Computeria**, 206 Long St, **T** 021-4265969 is open 24 hours and offers 10 mins for R5. There are also internet cafés in all the shopping centres, including Victoria Wharf at the Waterfront.

Left luggage

There is a left-luggage facility at the train station on Adderely St next to Platform 24.

Libraries

The main library is the **South African Public Library** on Queen Victoria St, **T** 021-4246320, www.ulsa.ac.za. There are also a number of local libraries found in the suburbs to which visitors can obtain temporary membership cards.

Lost property

Check the 'lost and found' section in the classified section of the daily newspapers. Report your loss at the local police station and leave a contact telephone number and address.

Motorcycle hire

South African Motorcycle Tours, Sierra Cottage, Gemini Way, Constantia, **T** 021-7947887, www.sa-motorcycle-tours.com.

! South Africa's 'Unofficial National Flower' is the plastic
• carrier bag. Such huge numbers are snagged in every tree and fence in the city, that you now have to pay for them in supermarkets and there are plans to make them illegal.

Media

Cape Town has an English morning paper, the **Cape Times**, and an evening paper, the **Argus**. Both are good sources of what's going on in the city, with daily listings and entertainment sections. There is also a daily paper in Afrikaans, **Die Burger** and **Xhosa**. As for the radio, **Radio KFM: 94.5 FM**, contemporary music, mix of old classics and new hits. **Good Hope FM: 94-97 FM**, teenage pop music, current hits. **Lotus FM: 97.8 FM**, general Indian affairs and Bollywood music.

Medical services

Dentists and doctors are listed in the telephone directory under Dental or Medical Practitioner or ask at your hotel reception. See also Dentists, and Hospitals, above and Pharmacies below.

Pharmacies

Emergency pharmacies include: **Glengariff Link Max**, 2 Main Rd, Sea Point, **T** 021-4348622; **Lite-Kem**, 24 Darling St, **T** 021-4618040.

Post

The **General Post Office** is between Parliament and Plein sts by the Golden Acre shopping centre. Post restante is in the main hall, open 0800-1630, Sat 0800-1200. There is a separate entrance for parcels in Plein St. Post offices are found in all the suburbs close to the principal shopping centres. Courier service, Citi-Sprint is on 105 Strand St, **T** 021-4247131.

Public holidays

Jan 1 – New Years Day; Mar 21 – Human Rights Day; Good Friday; Family Day (Easter Monday); Apr 27 – Freedom Day; May 1 – Worker's Day; Jun 16 – Youth Day; Aug 9 – National Women's Day; Sep 24 – Heritage Day; Dec 16 – Day of Reconciliation; Dec 25 – Christmas Day; Dec 26 – Day of Goodwill.

Religious services
Anglican, St George's Cathedral, **T** 021-424 7360.
Buddhist, **T** 021-6853371. **Dutch Reformed**, **T** 021-4249131.
Jewish, Cape Town Hebrew Congregation, **T** 021-4651405.
Muslim, Muslim Judicial Council (0830-1300), **T** 021-6965150.
Roman Catholic, St Mary's Cathedral, **T** 021-4611167.

Student organizations
ISTC, www.isic.org **University of Cape Town**, www.uct.ac.za

Telephone
International operator, **T** 0009. **Local enquiries**, **T** 1023.
Postnet is a useful chain found throughout the city, usually in shopping malls. The main branch is in the Union Castle Building, 6 Hout St, **T** 021-4260179, www.postnet.co.za. Services include sending parcels, internet, fax sending and receiving, phonecards, passport photos. Open Mon-Fri 0830-1700, Sat 0830-1300.

Time
South Africa's time zone is +2 GMT. It is two hours ahead of the UK and Ireland, one hour ahead of the rest of Europe, seven hours ahead of east coast America and eight hours behind Australia.

Toilets
Standard European-style toilets. There is a dearth of public toilets in Cape Town, although all museums, sights, and of course, bars and restaurants have public toilet facilities.

Transport enquiries
Baz Bus, 8 Rosedene Rd, Sea Point, **T** 021-4392323, www.bazbus.com **Blue Train**, **T** 021-4482672, www.bluetrain.co.za **Golden Arrow**, **T** 021-9378800, www.gabs.co.za **Greyhound**, 1 Adderley St, **T** 021-5056363, www.greyhound.co.za **Intercape**, **T** 0861287287,

www.intercape.co.za **Metrorail**, **T** 0800-656463. **Spoornet**,
www.spoornet.co.za **Translux**, **T** 021- Translux, **T** 011-7743333,
www.translux.co.za

Travel agents
Pentravel, Claremont, **T** 021-6704000, www.pentravel.co.za
STA Travel, 31 Riebeeck St, **T** 021-4186570, www.statravel.co.za
Sure Travel, offices around the city, **T** 0861-676869,
www.suretravel.co.za **Rennies Travel** (Thomas Cook
representatives), 2 St George's Mall, **T** 021-4181206,
www.renniestravel.co.za

A sprint through history

2,000 BC	First evidence of human inhabitants in the Cape.
1 AD	Nomadic San people in area replaced by semi-nomadic Khoi groups.
1503	António de Saldanha, a Portuguese admiral, lands in Table Bay.
1503-10	Portuguese attempt bartering with Khoi, but relations remain hostile.
Late 1500s	British and Dutch mariners begin using the Cape to restock boats.
1652	Dutch attempt to settle in the Cape; Jan van Riebeeck lands in Table Bay.
Late 1600s	Dutch East India Company (Vereenigde Oost-Indische Compagnie or VOC). Expands settlement; Khoi are driven further out and first slaves imported from Indonesia and West Africa.
1679	Governor Simon van der Stel arrives in the Cape and begins rapid expansion. Soon founds settlement at Stellenbosch.
1688	French Protestant Huguenot refugees arrive in the Cape; most are moved to area around Stellenbosch to encourage wine production.
1780	Dutch fight the Xhosa at Great Fish River.
1795	France invades Holland, prompting the British to seize the Cape following the Battle of Muizenberg.
1803	Treaty of Amiens restores the Cape to the Batavian Republic of the Netherlands.

1806	British take control again with the resumption of the Anglo-French wars.
1825	Industrialization in Europe brings great changes to Cape Town. First steamship, the *Enterprise,* arrives in Table Bay in October.
1836	The Dutch settlers (Boer) find British administration unfavourable. Great Trek begins as they look to the interior for land.
1860	Construction begins on Victoria & Alfred Basins.
1867	Gold found at Witwatersrand.
1899-1902	Anglo-Boer war. Boers surrender in 1902.
1910	Act of Union between British colonies and Boer republics comes into being. Issues such as dual official languages are resolved, while the matter of African political rights is sidestepped. First signs of African nationalism.
1912	First meeting of the African Native National Congress, later the African National Congress (ANC).
1913	Natives Land Act prevents blacks from owning more than 7.5% of all land.
1920s	Rise in Afrikaner nationalism.
1930s	Afrikaans takes over from Dutch as an official language.
1935	Voting rights removed from last black faction (property holders in the Western Cape).

World War II	South Africa brought into the war by Prime Minister Jan Smuts in support of the British.
1948	National Party voted in with new racist ideology of apartheid. Racial laws such as forbidding interracial marriage begin to be passed.
1952	Start of the ANC's Defiance Campaign using Gandhian tactics of peaceful resistance.
1955	ANC draws up and adopts Freedom Charter.
1959	Pan African Congress (PAC) splits from ANC under leadership of Robert Sobukwe. Massive anti-pass law campaign is launched.
1960	Sharpville massacre, followed by nationwide (black) riots and strikes. State of Emergency declared; ANC and PAC banned.
1961	South Africa leaves the British Commonwealth and becomes a Republic. Organized armed wing of the ANC, Umkhonto we Sizwe (Spear of the Nation), is formed.
1963	Nelson Mandela jailed for life.
Early 1970s	South Africa Students Organization (SASO) formed under leadership of Steve Biko.
1976	Beginning of the Soweto Uprising.
1977	Steve Biko murdered.
1982	Formation of the United Democratic Front (UDF), a union of community, non-governmental and church organizations with strong links to the ANC. UDF spearheads protest throughout the 1980s.

1985	State of Emergency declared. State-sponsored murder and torture widespread; political riots and unrest escalate.
1990	Ban lifted on ANC and PAC. Nelson Mandela freed.
1994	South Africa's first democratic elections held; Nelson Mandela sworn in as president.
Mid 1990s	Truth and Reconciliation Commission, chaired by Desmond Tutu, begins hearings to encourage national healing. Violence escalates in KwaZulu Natal between ANC and Inkharta Freedom Party (IFP).
1996	First democratic constitution passed by the Constitutional Assembly in 1996.
1999	Mandela stands down following successful elections and is succeeded by Thabo Mbeki.
2000-01	Mbeki comes under intense criticism due to his scepticism of the link between HIV and AIDS, despite South Africa being in the throes of one of the world's worst AIDS endemics.
2002	Half a million South African children are identified as AIDs orphans. Johannesburg hosts the World Summit on Sustainable Development.
2003	JM Coetzee wins the Nobel Prize for Literature.
2004	South Africa celebrates a decade of democracy. Thabo Mbeki's government begins distributing free antiretroviral drugs to HIV/AIDS sufferers. The ANC wins the March 2004 General Election with a landslide. South Africa is awarded the 2010 football World Cup – the first African nation to host the tournament.

Cape Jazz

The decade following the Second World War was the great era of jazz in South Africa, a time of significant artistic development for the country, but also a period of devastating social upheaval with the rise of apartheid.

Jazz was seen as much more than a musical style – it represented an urbanized sophistication that flew in the face of prevailing apartheid ideology. Pan-tribalist and resolutely optimistic, jazz acted as a useful vehicle for a subtle form of reaction to the draconian workings of the state. A cutting-edge Americanized culture took hold in many townships, where types of dress, language and music were adopted as the ultimate opposition to the lifestyle encouraged by the government.

South African jazz became known as Marabi, with its roots in the Maraba township in Pretoria. While much of South Africa's better-known jazz developed around Johannesburg, famously represented by the socially vital magazine *Drum*, most jazz musicians and their audiences came from similar urban backgrounds, and a different scene began to flourish in Cape Town.

Although earlier African-American music was influenced by visiting American musicians, no jazz artists toured South Africa until the mid-1950s. Instead, inspiration was transmitted mostly through film and recorded music. Cape Town, however, had the advantage of being a port, and much of the vibrant scene there is attributed to the incoming influence of American sailors.

Not only did visiting sailors bring records and movies, but some of the battleships that docked in Cape Town had jazz bands on board, and new sounds spread quickly from the docks to the townships. But Cape Town's township jazz bands were not content with merely copying what they heard – instead, they combined the sounds of American swing with African beats and improvisation, creating a unique fusion which became known as Cape Jazz.

Arguably the godfather of Cape Jazz is pianist Abdullah Ibrahim, also known as Dollar Brand. Born in Cape Town in 1934, Dollar was brought up on traditional African songs, religious music and jazz, and became a professional musician in 1949, playing with the Tuxedo Slickers and Willie Max Big Band. In the late 1950s he joined Hugh Masekela, Jonas Gwanga and Kippie Moeketsi to become a central figure in South Africa's progressive jazz movement, which took its lead from New York-based sounds. They formed the Jazz Epistles, cut a ground-breaking record and performed to international critical acclaim at the first Cold Castle National Jazz Festival in 1960.

The heady days of the late 50s and early 60s soon came to an end, however, and Cape Jazz, like so many other forms of cultural expression, was slowly strangled by the state. Following the Sharpeville massacre, the cultural boycott, ludicrous radio restrictions and police bannings, many of the key players left South Africa, mainly for Europe and US. However, a handful of well-known artists stayed, including the late Basil Coetzee, born in District Six and first gaining musical credit with Ibrahim. Coetzee remained in South Africa after the departure of many of his colleagues, and weathered the lean years working in a shoe factory. He was re-joined by prominent saxophonist Robbie Jansen in the early-1980s and so began a new chapter in Cape Jazz. A group of musicians, headed by Jansen and Coetzee, performed throughout the turbulent period of 1985-90, mostly at political and cultural events across the country, cementing the key role of music in the anti-apartheid struggle.

Meanwhile, exiled musicians continued to expand the genre abroad, and at the end of apartheid many of the original creators of Cape Jazz returned. The scene is once again flourishing. Old-timers such as Ibrahim and Jansen continue to dominate, although new influences, both from abroad and around South Africa, are once again changing the face of Cape Jazz. Yet its vital elements will always remain – both as a form of musical expression and cultural demonstration.

Books

Literature

South Africa has produced a number of internationally recognized and award-winning novelists. Probably the best known is **John Coetzee**, winner of the 2003 Nobel Prize for Literature, whose novels include *Dusklands*, *In the Heart of the Country*, *Waiting for the Barbarians*, *Life & Times of Michael K* (winner of the 1983 Booker Prize), *Age of Iron*, *Foe* and *The Master of Petersburg*. He won the Booker Prize again in 1999 for his novel, *Disgrace*. His style is stark and intellectual, but surprisingly accessible, and he remains one of the most brilliant modern commentators on the lasting effects of apartheid.

Another award-winning South African novelist is **Nadine Gordimer**. Her novels include *A Guest of Honour*, *The Conservationist* (winner of the 1974 Booker Prize), *Burger's Daughter*, *July's People*, *A Sport of Nature*, *My Son's Story* and *None to Accompany Me*. Her beautifully written work tends to concentrate on the way wider political/social events impact on individual lives.

Bessie Head is a third widely respected South African author, though much of her work is set in Botswana where she was exiled in 1964. She wrote three novels – *When Rain Clouds Gather*, *Maru* and the semi-autobiographical *A Question of Power*, a collection of short-stories *The Collection of Treasures*, and a portrait of the Botswanan village where she lived and eventually died at the age of just 49, *Serowe, The Village of the Rain-wind*.

Andre Brink is another internationally recognized South African author who has published in both English and Afrikaans. His novels in English include *A Chain of Voices*, *The Ambassador*, *Looking on Darkness*, *Rumours of Rain*, *An Act of Terror* and *A Dry White Season* (made into a Hollywood film). Like Coetzee he has published extensively on literary criticism as well as his own fiction.

All of these authors are highly recommended though their work is not always easy going – especially Head's *A Question of Power*.

Tom Sharpe, a Englishman who lived in South Africa throughout the 1950s, represents a very different literary genre from the books mentioned above. His two South African novels *Riotous Assembly* and *Indecent Exposure* are both hilarious, especially because the absurd and grotesque situations and characters he conjures up seem eminently believable in the South African context.

Another South African novelist, representing a previous generation, is **Alan Paton**, internationally recognized and loved by many (though others find him overly sentimental). He is best known for his novel *Cry the Beloved Country* but he also published two others – *Too Late the Phalarope* and *Ah, But Your Land is Beautiful*, a collection of short stories *Debbie Go Home* and many works of non-fiction.

Another well-known South African novel is **Olive Schreiner**'s *The Story of an African Farm*. When it was first published in 1883 (under the pseudonym Ralph Iron) it received notoriety for its feminist and anti-racist message. **Rider Haggard**, who published his hugely popular *King Solomon's Mines* two years after Schreiner published *The Story of an African Farm*, covered very different subjects. The romantic theme of his novels with an African setting, such as *King Solomon's Mines* and *She*, remain popular today. They are certainly better written and more exciting than their modern counterparts of the Wilbur Smith variety.

The majority of the internationally recognized South African novelists described above are white. This does not mean, however, that there is not a tradition of novel writing amongst South Africa's African, Coloured and Indian populations. The two earliest African novelists in the country were **RRR Dhlomo**, who wrote *An African Tragedy*, first published in 1928 and **Sol Plaatje**, who wrote *Mhudi*, completed in 1917 but not published until 1930. During the apartheid years, however, many Africans concentrated on more overtly political writings than novels. Some of these are outlined below.

Short stories have also been a fairly popular form of literature: interesting collections include *Hungry Flames and other Black South African Short Stories*, edited by Mbulelo Mzamane, Harlow, Longman, 1986 and *The Penguin Book of Contemporary South African Short Stories*, edited by Stephen Gray, London, Penguin, 1993.

Autobigraphy and political writing

The autobiography that has received most attention is, not surprisingly, **Nelson Mandela**'s *Long Walk to Freedom*, (London, Little Brown, 1994), a fascinating, if at times heavy-going, insight to the struggle. A number of other ANC leaders have also published autobiographies, including a posthumous publication by **Joe Slovo**, *Slovo: the unfinished autobiography*, (Randburg, Ravan Press, 1995). Previous generations of African leaders also published autobiographies including **ZK Matthews** *Freedom for my People: Southern Africa 1901-1968*, edited by Monica Wilson, (London, Collins, 1981), and **Clements Kadalie** *My Life and the ICU: the Autobiography of a Black Trade Unionist in South Africa*, edited by Stanley Trapido, (London, Cassell, 1970). A recent best-seller is **Desmond Tutu's** *No Future Without Forgiveness*, (Image Books, 2000), a fascinating and often harrowing account of his role as Chairman of the Truth and Reconciliation Committee in the late 1990s. Autobiographies tracing the lives of less famous South Africans include two volumes from **Ezekiel Mphahlele** *Down Second Avenue* and *Afrika my Music: an Autobiography*, (Johannesburg, Ravan Press, 1984), *Bloke Modisane Blame me on History*, (London, Penguin, 1990), and the highly recommended *Call me Woman* by **Ellen Kuzwayo**, (London, Women's Press, 1985). There have also been a number of collections of political speeches, articles and other writing by major political figures such as **Steve Biko**'s *I Write what I Like*, edited by Aelred Stubbs, (Edinburgh, Heinemann, 1987). Others have published diaries written while in prison, such as **Albie Sachs**'s *The Jail Diary of Albie Sachs*, (London, Paladin, 1990). Another interesting diary is **Sol Plaatje**'s *Mafeking Diary: a Black Man's View of a White Man's War*, edited by John L Comaroff, (Johannesburg, Southern Book Publishers, 1989).

History and biography
Many readers find that history comes alive more through biography than through general textbooks. Recommended and widely available biographies include: **Peter Alexander**'s biography of the South African novelist and well-known liberal Alan Paton, *Alan Paton*, (Oxford, OUP, 1994); **William Hancock**'s two volume biography of *Jan Smuts, The Sanguine Years, 1870-1919* and *The Fields of Force 1919-1950* (Cambridge, CUP, 1962 and 1968); **Richard Mendelsohn**'s biography of the businessman Sammy Marks, *Sammy Marks* (Cape Town, David Philip, 1991); **Antony Thomas**'s book on Cecil Rhodes, *Rhodes: The Face for Africa* (Johannesburg, Jonathan Ball, 1996); **Donald Woods**' book on Steve Biko – the basis for the film 'Cry Freedom' – *Biko* (London, Paddington Press, 1978); **Ruth First**'s biography of the late 19th/early 20th-century novelist, feminist and anti-racism campaigner Olive Schreiner, *Olive Schreiner* (London, Women's Press, 1989); and finally **Brian Willan** on Sol Plaatje, the novelist and early African nationalist, *Sol Plaatje: South African Nationalist 1876-1932* (London, Heinemann, 1984). Biography tends to be associated with the lives of 'great men': one that is not is **Charles Van Onselen**'s *The Seed is Mine: the Life of Kas Maine, a South African Sharecropper, 1894-1985* (Oxford, James Curry,1996) – it is a long book but fascinating and highly recommended.

Natural history and environment
Good guides to game parks, wildlife and natural history include: **Jean Dorst** and **Pierre Dandelot** *A Field Guide to the Larger Mammals of Africa* (London, Collins); **Gordon Maclean**

Roberts' *Birds of South Africa* (Cape Town, CTP); **CW Mackworth-Praed** and **CHB Grant** *Birds of the Southern third of Africa* (London, Longman, 1963) and **Eve Palmer** *Field Guide to the Trees of Southern Africa* (London, Collins, 1977). Three general books on the South African environment and environmental problems are: **Mamphela Ramphela** (ed) *Restoring the Land* (London, Panos, 1991), **Jacklyn Cock** and **Eddie Koch** (eds) *Going Green: People, Politics and the Environment in South Africa* (Cape Town, OUP, 1991) and **Munyaradzi Chenje** and **Phyllis Johnson** (eds) *State of the Environment in Southern Africa* (Harare, SARDC, 1994).

Language

There are 11 official languages in South Africa. Throughout the country English is widely spoken and understood. About 60% of white South Africans, and most of the coloured community in Cape Town, speak Afrikaans. The majority of black South Africans in Cape Town speak Xhosa.

You will find that most people are bilingual, and road signs, for example, alternate between being in Afrikaans and English. There are a few pockets where only Afrikaans is spoken, but people should understand enough English to meet your needs. Nevertheless, it is always worth making the effort to learn a few words of Afrikaans or Xhosa – people are generally delighted that you've made the effort.

! There are few Afrikaans words you'll hear more than 'lekker' – used by people of every background and meaning 'nice', 'cool', 'tasty' or 'good'. It's applicable to anything from a meal to a holiday or a movie.

English	Afrikaans	Xhosa
hello	hallo	Molo (good morning)
		Rhoananai (good evening)
how are you?	hoe gaan dit?	kunjani?
please	asseblief	nceda
thank you	dankie	enkosi
yes	ja	ewe
no	nee	hayi
excuse me	verskoon my	uxolo
do you speak English?	praat u Engels?	uyakwazi ukuthetha siNgesi?

Useful words

apteek	chemist/pharmacy
berg	mountain
biltong	cured meat
boerwors	spicy sausage
braai	South African equivalent of a barbecue
burg	a term referring to a borough
dorp	a small country settlement where a road crosses a dry river bed
jol	party
kerk	church
lekker	good/nice
middestad	city centre
polisie	police
rooinek	literally 'redneck', a disparaging term used to describe English-speaking white South Africans
staad	city
strand	beach
uitgang	exit
veld	field
vlei	low lying lake or swamp
wyn	wine

Index

Credits

Footprint credits

Editor: Sophie Blacksell
Editorial assistant: Angus Dawson
Map editor: Sarah Sorensen

Publisher: Patrick Dawson
Series created by: Rachel Fielding
In-house cartography: Claire Benison,
Kevin Feeney, Robert Lunn
Proof-reading: Amanda Jones

Design: Mytton Williams
Maps: Footprint Handbooks Ltd

Photography credits

Front cover: Indexstock (tribal masks)
Inside: Francisca Kellett
(p1 Clock Tower, p5 Cape Argus Cycle
Tour, p29 Chapman's Peak Drive)
Generic images: John Matchett
Back cover: Francisca Kellett
(wine barrels)

Print

Manufactured in Italy by LegoPrint

Footprint feedback

We try as hard as we can to make
each Footprint guide as up to date as
possible but, of course, things always
change. If you want to let us know
about your experiences – good, bad
or ugly – then, don't delay, go to
www.footprintbooks.com and send
in your comments.

® Footprint Handbooks and the Footprint
mark are a registered trademark of
Footprint Handbooks Ltd

Publishing information

Footprint Cape Town
2nd edition
Text and maps
© Footprint Handbooks Ltd July 2004

ISBN 1 904777 21 X
CIP DATA: a catalogue record for this
book is available from the British Library

Published by Footprint
6 Riverside Court
Lower Bristol Road
Bath, BA2 3DZ, UK
T +44 (0)1225 469141
F +44 (0)1225 469461
discover@footprintbooks.com
www.footprintbooks.com

Distributed in the USA by
Publishers Group West

Complete title list

Latin America & the Caribbean

Argentina
Barbados (P)
Bolivia
Brazil
Caribbean Islands
Central America & Mexico
Chile
Colombia
Costa Rica
Cuba
Cusco & the Inca Trail
Dominican Republic
Ecuador & Galápagos
Guatemala
Havana (P)
Mexico
Nicaragua
Peru
Rio de Janeiro
South American Handbook
Venezuela

North America

New York (P)
Vancouver (P)
Western Canada

Middle East

Dubai (P)
Israel
Jordan
Syria & Lebanon

Africa

Cape Town (P)
East Africa
Egypt
Libya
Marrakech (P)
Morocco
Namibia
South Africa
Tunisia
Uganda

Asia

Bali
Bangkok & the Beaches
Cambodia
Goa
Hong Kong (P)
India
Indian Himalaya
Indonesia
Laos
Malaysia
Myanmar (Burma)
Nepal
North Pakistan
Pakistan
Rajasthan & Gujarat
Singapore
South India
Sri Lanka
Sumatra
Thailand
Tibet
Vietnam

Australasia

Australia
New Zealand
Sydney (P)
West Coast Australia

Europe

Andalucía
Barcelona (P)
Berlin (P)
Bilbao (P)
Bologna (P)
Cardiff (P)
Copenhagen (P)
Croatia
Dublin (P)
Edinburgh (P)
England
Glasgow (P)
Ireland
London
London (P)
Madrid (P)
Naples (P)
Northern Spain
Paris (P)
Reykjavík (P)
Scotland
Scotland Highlands & Islands
Seville (P)
Spain
Tallinn (P)
Turin (P)
Turkey
Valencia (P)
Verona (P)

Lifestyle

Surfing Europe

(P) denotes pocket guide

Advertising

245

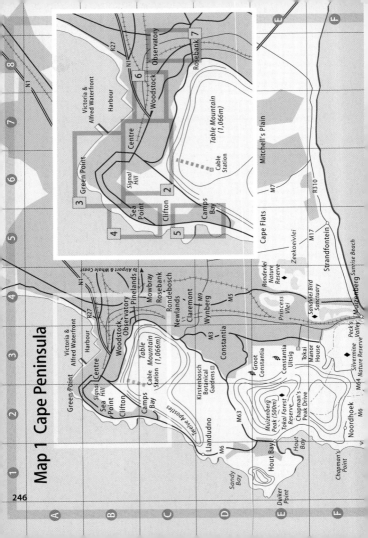

Map 1 Cape Peninsula

246

Green Point
Victoria & Alfred Waterfront
Harbour
Centre
Signal Hill
Sea Point
Camps Bay
Clifton
Twelve Apostles
Llandudno
Sandy Bay
Hout Bay
Duiker Point
Chapman's Point
Noordhoek
M6
Woodstock, Observatory
Table Mountain (1,066m)
Cable Station
Kirstenbosch Botanical Gardens
Muizenberg Peak (500m)
Tokai Forest Reserve
Chapman's Peak Drive
Groot Constantia
Constantia Uitsig
Tokai Manor House
Silvermine Nature Reserve Valley
M64
M6
M63
N1
To Airport & Whale Coast
Mowbray
Rosebank
Rondebosch
Newlands
Claremont
Wynberg
M9
M5
M3
Constantia
Princess Vlei
Rondevlei Nature Reserve
Sandvlei Bird Sanctuary
Peck's Valley
Zeekoeivlei
Strandfontein
Cape Flats
Muizenberg Sunrise Beach
M7
M17
R310
Mitchell's Plain

Inset map

3
Green Point
Victoria & Alfred Waterfront
Harbour
Centre
Signal Hill
Sea Point
Camps Bay
Clifton
4
2
5
Woodstock
Observatory
Rosebank
Table Mountain (1,066m)
Cable Station
6
7
R27
N1

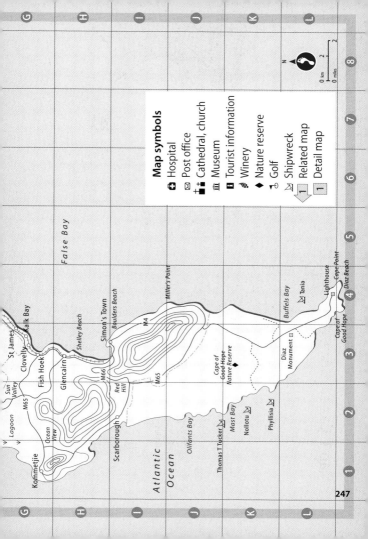

Map symbols

✚ Hospital
⊠ Post office
⚏ Cathedral, church
🏛 Museum
ℹ Tourist information
🍇 Winery
◆ Nature reserve
⛳ Golf
⚓ Shipwreck
🔽1 Related map
1 Detail map

N

0 km   2
0 miles   2

False Bay

St James
Kalk Bay
Clovelly
Sun Valley
Lagoon
Ocean View
Kommetjie
Fish Hoek
Glencairn
Shelley Beach
Simon's Town
Boulders Beach
Miller's Point
M4
M66
Red Hill
M65
Scarborough
Olifants Bay
Mast Bay
⚓ Thomas T Tucker
⚓ Nolloth
⚓ Phyllisia
Cape of Good Hope Nature Reserve
Diaz Monument
Buffels Bay
⚓ Tania
Cape of Good Hope
Lighthouse
Cape Point
⚓ Diaz Beach

Atlantic Ocean

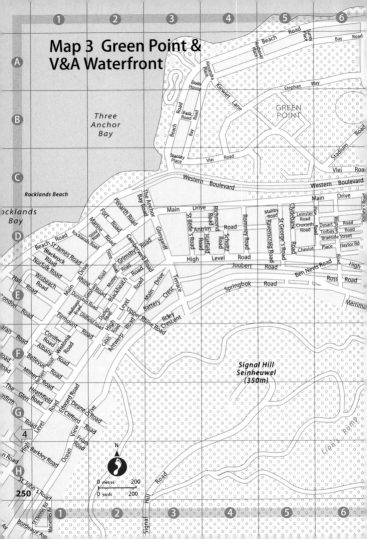

Map 3 Green Point & V&A Waterfront

Granger Bay

8

Beach Road

A

Metropolitan
Golf Course

Victoria Wharf

B

Sonnenberg Road

Granger Street

Victoria Basin

Union Castle Building

Fort Wynyard Road

Road

Time Ball Tower

V & A Hotel

Clock Tower

C

Portswood Road

Two Oceans Aquarium

Alfred Basin

West Road

South Arm

D

Duncan Dock

Western Boulevard

Main Drive

Fish Market

Ashsroad Road

Glenroy

Vreffereid Road

Cavalcade Road

Braemar Road

Hillside Terrace

Gallows Hill Road

Road

Duncan Road

E

Thornhill Road

Wessels Road

Berrand Road

Highfield Street

Cardiff Street

Western

Port

Road

Chepstow Road

Boundary Road

Ebenezer

Battery Street

Road

Carreg Crescent

Strand Street

De Smit Street

Liddie Street

Coburn Street

Sonnerset Street

Boulevard

Stanley Street

F

James Street

Napier Street

Alfred Street

Hospital Street

Ella Street

Dixon Street

Chiappini Street

Steytler Avenue

Longmarket Street

Strand Vos Street

Hudson Street

Mechau Street

Wharf Street

Jetty Street

Square

G

Military Road

August Street

Yusuf Drive

Hillgers Street

Prestwich Str

Hans Strijdom Avenue

Roggebaai

Bloem Road

Dawes Str

Signal Street

Riebeeck Street

Bree Street

Loop Street

Riebeeck Lane

Addeley Street

Riebeeck Statue

H

Avanu Street

Chiappini Street

Rose Street

Buitengracht Street

Castle Street

Hout Street

Waterkant Street

Pentz Road

Shortmarket Street

Longmarket Street

Church Street

Koopmans De Wet House

251

Upper Leeu

Dorp Lane

Bo-Kaap Museum

Church Street

Wal Street

The Pinnacle

Upper Per

Railway Station

Map 4 Sea Point

Rocklands Bay

Atlantic Ocean

Graaffs' Pool

N

0 metres 200
0 yards 200

A
B
C
D
E
F
G
H

1 2 3 4 5 6

Beach St
Blackhill Road
Norfolk Road
Wibsech Road
Hall Road
Aurora Lane
London Road
Conifer Road
Marais Road
Albany Road
Oliver Road
Ellis Road
Bellevue Road
Milton Road
Milner Road
Graham Road
Worcester Road
The Glen Road
Holmfirth Road
Heathfield Road
Arthur's Drive
Level Road
St. Main Road
Road
St. John's Road
Duncan Road
High Road
Barkley Road
Irwinton Road
Church Road
Clarens Road
Gorleston Road
Algakirk Road
St. John's Road
Monastery Road
Surf Street
St. Andrews Road
Francais Avenue
Beach Road
Casell Regent Road
Upper Road
Hanover Road
Chateau Av.
Bordeaux Avenue
Solomons Road
Quantok Road
Kei Apple Road
Normandie Road
De L'Hermite Avenue
Kloof Road
Kei Apple Grove
Quendon Road
Disandt Avenue
De Longueville Avenue
Sueur Avenue
Avenue
Kings Road
Alexander Road
Des Huguenots Avenue
Level Avenue
High Avenue
Chales Avenue
Queen's Road
Alexander Park
Craigrownie
Fresnaye Avenue
Protea Avenue
Disandt Avenue
De Berange Avenue
Saunders Road
Rochester Road
La Croix Avenue
St. Louis Avenue
Bartholomew Avenue
Seacliffe Road
Fir Lane
Portman Road
St. Patrick Road
Princes Road
Barry Lane
Brompton Road
Alexandra Road
Bellwood Road
Chamanite Avenue
Brittany Avenue
St. Jeans Av.
Deauville Av.
Victoria Road
Florida Road
Bonglu Steps
Ravine
Gordon St.
Marina Av.
Ocean View Drive
De Wet Road
St. Clair Avenue
Deauville Av.
Saunders Rock/-rots
Atson Rd
De Wet Road
Ocean View Drive
Acadia Road
To St Road

252

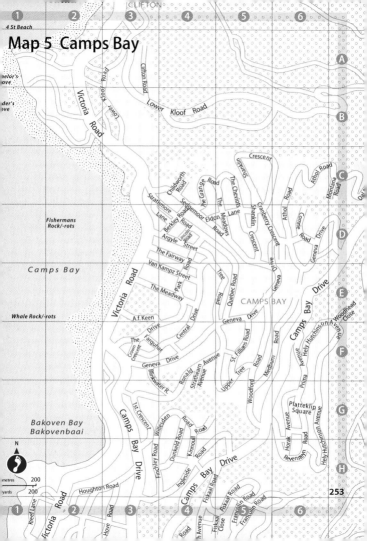

Map 5 Camps Bay

4 St Beach

chelor's
ove

der's
ove

Victoria Road

Lower Kloof Road

Clifton Road

Lower Kloof Road

Crescent

Shanklin

Childworth Road

Strathmore Lane

Berkley Road

Sedgemoor Road

The Grange Road

The Cheviots

Eldon Road

The Meadows

Cranberry Crescent

Athol Road

Montana Road

Dal

Game Road

Geneva Drive

Argyle Street

Lincoln Road

Fishermans
Rock/-rots

The Fairway Road

Van Kampz Street

Park Road

Peony

Tree

Quebec Road

Camps Bay

Geneva Drive

CAMPS BAY

Geneva Drive

Whale Rock/-rots

A.f. Keen

The Parquhat Drive

Central Drive

Crown Crescent

Geneva Drive

Blinkwater R.

Ronald Road

Strathearn Avenue

St. Fillians Road

Upper Tree

Woodford Road

Medburn Road

Camps Bay Drive

Hely Hutchinson Avenue

Woodhead Close

Prima Avenue

Bakoven Bay
Bakovenbaai

Camps Bay Drive

1st Crescent

Willesden Road

Dunkeld Road

Kimaall Road

Finchley Road

Ingleside Road

Camps Bay Drive

Platteklip
Square

Horak Avenue

Ravensem Road

Hely Hutchinson Avenue

N

metres   200
yards   200

Kreel Lane

Victoria Road

Hove Road

Houghton Road

Camps Bay Drive

Tikkah Avenue

Fiskaal Close

Fiskaal Road

Franklin Road

Franklin Road

Road

253

Map 6 Woodstock

254

Map 7 Observatory & Rosebank

Grote Schuur Drive

Groote Schuur Hospital

Amzio Road

Penzance Road

OBSERVATORY

Settlers Way

Union Place

MOWBRAY

Rhodes Drive

Rhodes Drive

ROSEBANK

Woolsack Drive

University of Cape Town

255

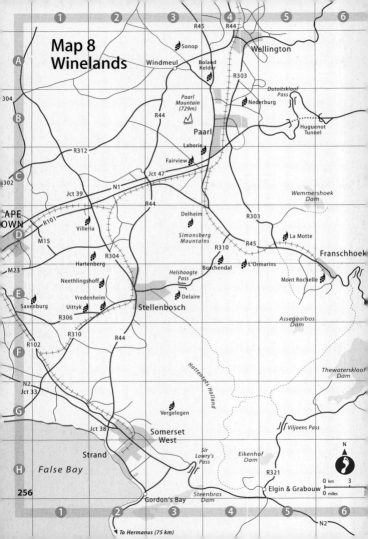